Ship Models from Kits

Le Hussard, c1848

Ship Models
from Kits

Colin Riches

Model Expo
Publications, Inc.

To Sylvia, my best critic.

All photographs by John McKay, Hull.

First published in Great Britain in 1984 by Conway Maritime Press Ltd, 24 Bride Lane, Fleet Street, London
EC4Y 8DR
Reprinted 1986

Published in the USA by Model Expo Publications, Inc, 23 Just Road, Fairfield, NJ 07007.

Manufactured in Great Britain.

Contents

Preface

This book is dedicated to all those 'kitchen table top' modelmakers who, having bought their kit, become frustrated, through one reason or another, during the making of it.

Lack of knowledge, inadequate instructions, missing pieces, etc, are all factors which spell disappointment to the would-be modelmaker. The aim of this book is to provide that knowledge by describing fully, using text and illustrations, each stage of the construction of a typical, medium-priced kit.

The use of expensive tools and equipment is **not** an essential part of the modelmaker's 'stock in trade', and all the work described is based upon this fact. Hints for building techniques and 'wangles', accumulated over the years, are included, and they all work! Gaining confidence in modelmaking is essential; hints for experimenting to gain this confidence are therefore also included.

The key to success in good modelmaking is always to experiment in building any particular part, and this book does not intend to suggest that the methods described are the only way; it should, however, prove an invaluable guide to both the beginner and to those modelmakers conditioned to any one method of construction.

The Model

The model featured within this book is of the **Le Hussard**. A French gun boat of 1848, she was armed with two carronades, which, due to their ability to move through an arc of approximately 300 degrees, gave the vessel a much more flexible way of concentrating firepower. By not having to rely on manoeuvring to bring a 'broadside' into use, the vessel could cause immense damage at a relatively far range. A fast brigantine-rigged vessel, she was used mainly in the coastal regions guarding vessels from the privateers who preyed upon the coastal traffic.

The model is simple to build, and each stage in the construction is described, with additional hints to aid the builder of a different model, or to allow the builder to alter the model to a ship of his (or her) choice.

All the photographs are of the model shown on the frontispiece. She was constructed using the techniques described in this book and the tools listed in Chapter 11. The result the reader may judge for himself!

Strange-sounding nautical terms are given a full, simple explanation. The building is outlined in stages and follows the normal building methods used by most kit manufacturers. Each section is complete within itself, and thus other sections may be tackled during delays caused by a part drying or setting, after glueing. Using this method, the modelmaker may complete his deck fittings, for instance, during the lengthy time it takes to build the hull. It also ensures the modelmaker will avoid rushing any one section and thus spoiling his model.

Each chapter should be studied completely, as other methods are described within. It will also be found that individual kits may differ slightly, and so different types of fittings are shown.

Constant reference to the kit instructions and plans is necessary, especially for measurement and position.

Chapter 1: The Kit

Having bought your kit, restrain your desire to start immediately! All too often the modelmaker will open up his new kit, select a few pieces – usually of the more obvious shapes – open a few packets, thereby losing some of the contents, and launch himself into the actual building! Two or three weeks later, having reached a critical point, he finds a piece missing. The delay in obtaining the replacement does nothing for his temper, spoils his enjoyment of his model, and ruins forever the manufacturer's reputation!

It is far better to use a methodical approach from the start. Gather together as many small containers as possible; these may be of clear plastic or margarine tubs, empty jam jars, etc. Open the kit, and, using the lid, systematically check **all** the contents. Count from the base of the box into the lid, using the parts list or instructions, and placing all the small items into the containers. Compile an accurate list of all the parts missing, and return the list to either the retailer, or to the manufacturer, giving as much information as possible. Do this as soon as possible, while the retailer remembers you! For example:

Part No. 67. Only one anchor included.

Checking the contents of the kit.

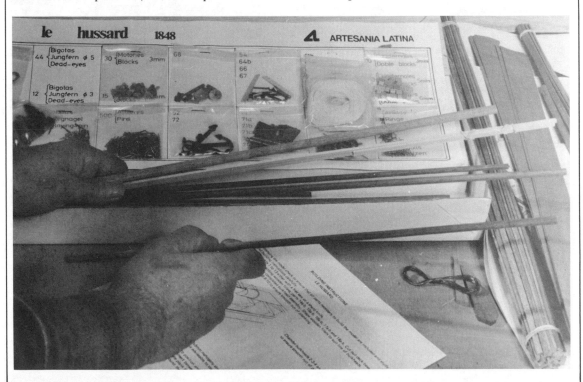

Part No. 24. Six (6) hull planks split and unusable.

Part No. 102. Two (2) pieces of 5mm dowel badly warped.

Check all the parts included during this first examination, and, additionally, match as many parts as possible to those on the plan drawing.

Some kits include a 'pre-check' list of parts for ease of checking. This will simplify the checking which now becomes a simple matter of counting the pieces of various woods in any particular bundle. Thus, if there are 32 pieces

of 5mm x 2mm x 490mm hull planks, on the list and in the bundle, all the pieces required during the construction are there.

Containers

The kit which has all the very small parts in plastic bags, usually on a larger card which gives the part numbers, can prove a hindrance. For some unaccountable reason, dogs enjoy the texture and taste of the parts included upon these cards!

Once the bags are opened, the danger of loss increases, and to ensure this does not happen, note the parts numbers, label a

Matching parts to plans.

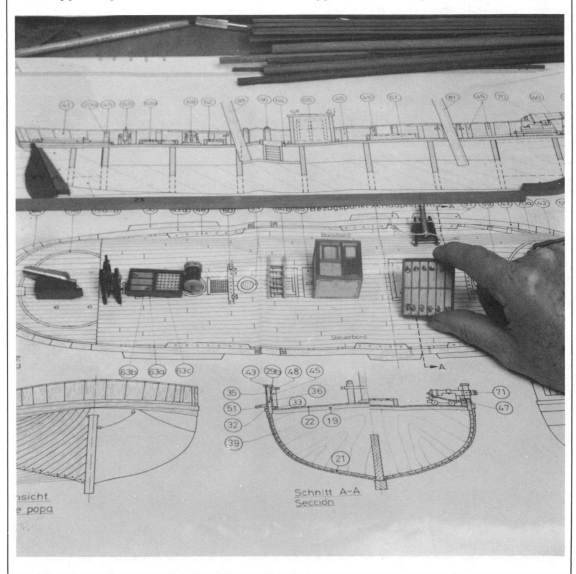

container and transfer the small parts to it, during the checking. Any deficiency should be noted and included in the list to the retailer.

In the majority of cases, the retailer will not carry a comprehensive stock to replenish your missing parts. He will, in turn, either have to contact the firm's representative, or the manufacturer, and some delay will inevitably occur. All manufacturers take great care to ensure that the contents are correct, but mistakes can happen. They will happily replace any missing parts; no manufacturer wants his reputation to be destroyed by a dissatisfied customer.

Checking parts into the containers.

Typical Kit Drawings

Plan

Elevation

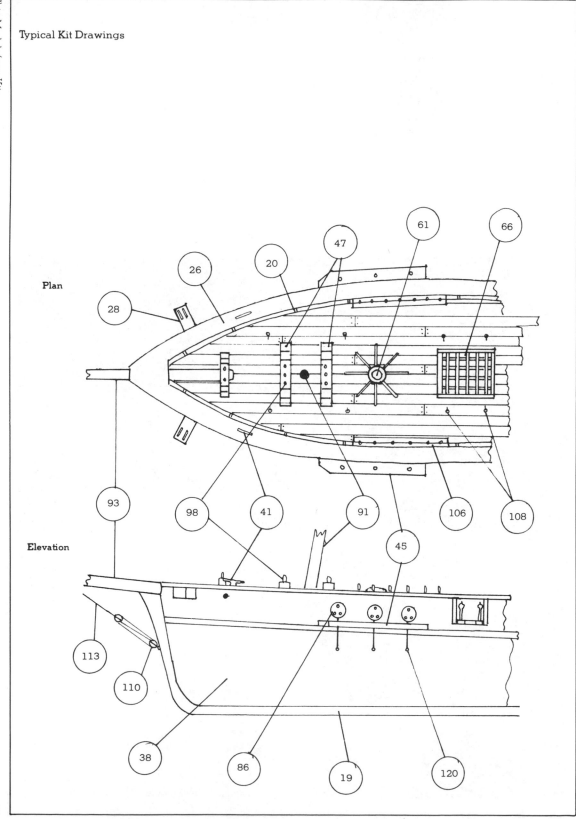

Chapter 2:
Plans & Drawings

Kit plans and drawings are produced to a high degree of quality and accuracy. In addition to the smaller 'exploded' views of the various fittings and assembly stages, which are usually not to scale, full size drawings are included.

These are of the ship viewed from the side (or plan) and from the top (or elevation), and should be to scale. These can be employed during the checking and identification of the kit contents, and when measuring items, both for size and shape. The position of ancillary equipment, such as eyebolts and cleats, etc, will also be given in their respective locations.

Numbers on the drawings corresponding to the parts list will also help you during identification and building, the position of the various parts being identified by means of pointers.

Rigging plans, giving the 'step-by-step' sequence, are usually included. These may be followed with confidence, as the sequence is invariably worked out during the building of the prototype model.

The importance of working from the plans cannot be stressed too much. The angles shown, the curves described, the final appearance, are all aspects which attracted you, the modelmaker, to the model in the first instance, and anything less than the model as shown will prove very disappointing!

Some typical drawings of actual kits are shown. Obviously these will vary from kit to kit, but, after comparing them, you should arrive at a better understanding of the parts, and their construction.

Some hints upon construction and method

Whatever stage you are at, whether building the initial framework of the hull, or assembling a foremast, approach the work in a methodical manner. Identify **all** the pieces required for the assembly, and, after cutting to size, replace all other parts of the model back into the box lid. If the assembly has to be put aside for the glue to set, or varnish to dry, isolate all the constituent parts with it. A clear plastic 'freezer' bag will prove helpful for smaller items. When assembling the larger items, such as the hull framework, or the planking, try to complete that stage before embarking on another.

You will find that it is better to use the time spent waiting for a part to dry by making the deck fittings, ensuring the holes in the deadeye blocks, etc, are clear, in fact, any of the numerous small jobs that need to be done. Consequently, when the next stage is reached the part will be already assembled, or finished, allowing better concentration on the actual fixing to the model. All small assemblies should be completed and varnished or painted, leaving only the surface to be glued in the natural wood state.

Typical kit section drawings.

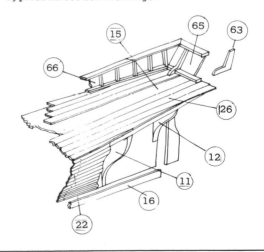

Scale

The majority of kits are models of actual ships, and the size of the model will depend upon the scale used. This is sometimes marked on the box lid, or plans, and is usually expressed as 1:48, or 1:50, etc. Put quite simply, 1:48, means the scale is 1/48th the size of the original, ie, one foot on the model represents 48ft on the original. As there are 48 quarter inches in each foot, the scale may be stated as 'one quarter scale' and each quarter inch on the model will represent one foot on the original ship. All other scales can be worked out in this manner. The drawing opposite will give a better idea exactly what this means in relation to your model.

The height of a door in a deckhouse **must** be sufficient for a scale figure to be able to get inside **without** hitting his head. Can he climb up the steps or ratlines on the rigging? Or would he – a very common fault on models – have to take a step the equivalent to climbing onto the kitchen table? These and other faults **do** occur, and can spoil the appearance of any model, however well built! Do keep the appearance of scale in mind **at all times**. Make a small template giving the size and

1:48 Scale deck planking.

shape of an average-sized man, and use it continuously to check. If no scale size is shown on the model, try to work out from a convenient door or ladder the approximate size, and work accordingly.

There are, however, occasions where to keep strictly to scale is not practical. The drawings relating to the appearance of deck planking is one of these. Planking was not laid on the sailing ships in one unbroken line; a convenient length, which varied from 6, 9 to 12ft, was employed. A common size for planking width was 4 or 6in. In the drawings illustrated, the approximate correct size planking would be the centre one, given a 1:48 scale. However assuming you want to represent the marking between the planks (described in Chapter 5) be warned the planking lines may rapidly become confused, and may even spoil the final appearance of the model.

I recommend that the planking strips within the model are used in the widths given, trimming the lengths to represent approximately 12ft. The finished appearance will be most satisfactory to all but the most critical of viewers, and their remarks will not be appreciated, anyway!

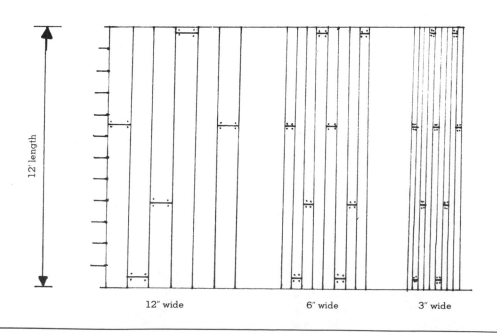

12' length

12" wide   6" wide   3" wide

Scale figures.

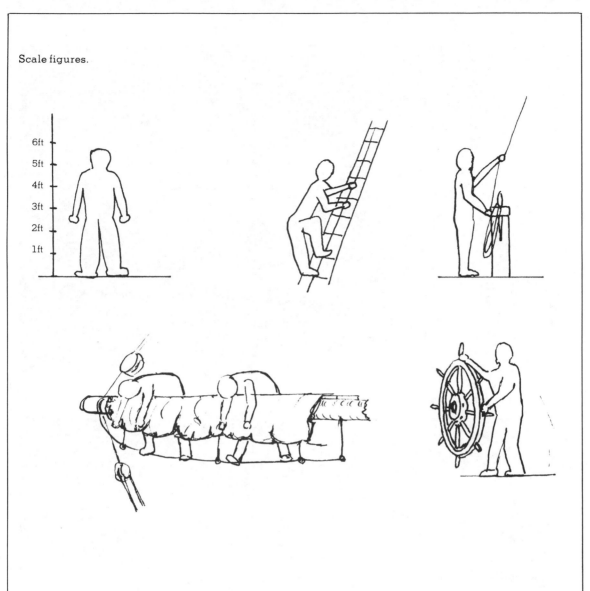

6ft
5ft
4ft
3ft
2ft
1ft

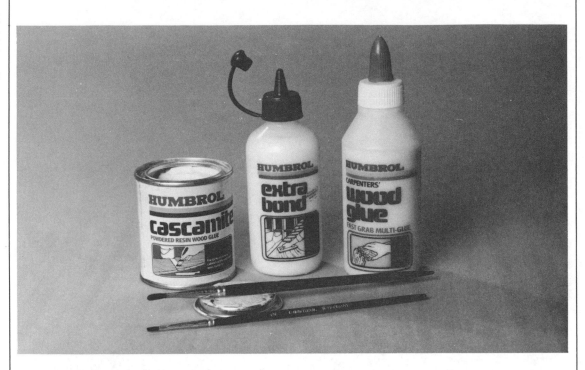

Cascamite, Extra Bond and carpenter's wood glue.

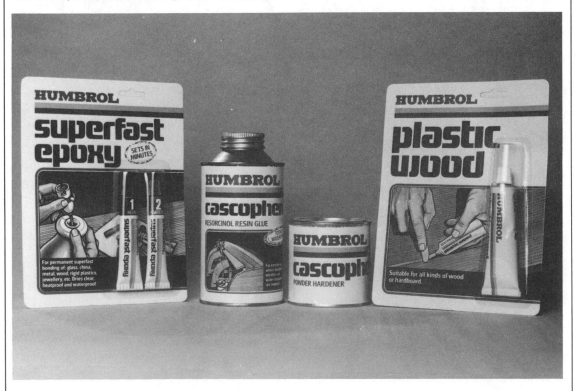

Superfast epoxy, cascophen and plastic wood.

Chapter 3: Glues, Paints & Varnishes

Glues

A wide range of glues are available today, many designed for specific work or materials. The modelmaker who works in wood rarely needs to enter this specialist field, being concerned mainly with the use of a glue which will, ideally, provide him with a good strong bond, a reasonably quick drying time, and does not leave a film over the joint or surface. Additionally, he may, for other work, require glues which will provide an 'instant' bond, or ones which will bond different materials (such as metal to wood, etc), and so the Humbrol range of adhesives are described.

The Superglue type of adhesive is **not** recommended for use in modelmaking. The possibility of small children, naturally interested in the creation of a model, picking up the container, whilst the modelmaker is occupied, is deterrent enough for any parent!

Woodworking adhesives

Carpenter's wood glue A 'fast grab', 'fast set' woodworking glue, of immense strength. With a nozzle for ease of application, it provides an ideal bond for all woods. Apply to both surfaces; any residue or overspill may be removed using a damp **not wet** cloth, before the glue has set. Ideal for fixing planks and the framework of the model.

Extra bond A woodworking glue which provides extra stength when needed. It is diluted with water and applied by brush. Ideal for those parts of a model which may be subjected to strain, such as the shroud tables or fife rails.

Cascamite A powdered, resin-type glue, which, when mixed with water, has a working life of approximately three hours. Applied by brush, it is ideal for fixing the hull planking, giving you time to rectify any mistakes before the glue has set.

Contact glues

As the name suggests, contact-type glues give instant (or almost instant), bonding between two surfaces pressed together – ideally for model work, there should be the facility to alter, or adjust, the part to its final position. Pressure should be maintained upon the joint whenever possible, and left overnight if the part has to bear any load, or strain. The bond is very strong, and is impossible to break without damage to the surrounding wood, so obviously great care is needed both in the marking of the proposed joint and the final position. The value of 'dry-fitting' such joints cannot be over-emphasised. Application is to both surfaces, which should be 'touch-dry', before the woods are placed together.

Superstick Adjustable contact glue, with a nozzle for ease of application. Slight 'pause' facility allows for final positioning of the parts.

Epoxy-type glues

These types of glue consist of two components, a resin base and a hardener. When mixed in equal quantities, a smooth paste is formed, with a working life of approximately five minutes. Consequently only sufficient quantity should be mixed to complete that portion of the work in hand. Epoxy-type glue is ideal for securing contrasting materials (brass to wood, metal to metal, etc), and is effective when securing ring-bolts into the deck, or cannon barrels to the carriages. It should be mixed on a piece of scrap card or wood, and the minimum amount

A range of paintbrushes commercially available.

possible applied. Use a small spatula, or matchstick. Drys to a clear, hard finish.

Superfast epoxy Both tubes come in a 'blister' pack and are clearly marked. Full instructions are given on the back of the pack.

Resin-type glues

These types of glues have a longer drying time and may be used in preference to any woodworking glue. The advantages are the additional strength gained, coupled with water-resistant properties, especially when used on a working, sailing model. Usually formed by mixing the resin base with a powdered hardener, it has a working life of between three and four hours, and provides immense strength. Applied by brush, there is no solvent known, once the glue has set, and any excess or spillage must be removed before this happens. Brushes can be cleaned by washing in warm, soapy water immediately after use.

Cascamite A powdered, water-based glue, already described.

Cascophen resorcinol resin Twin-pack, consisting of a resin base and a powdered hardener. Full instructions for mixing are given on the pack.

IMPORTANT

Whichever glues are used, the maker's instructions should be followed **exactly**. Some forms of resin glue may cause a rash, or dermatitis. They may also give off an inflammable vapour, and there should be adequate ventilation during their usage. **Avoid all** contact with the skin and eyes, and wash hands immediately, after use.

Plastic wood This comes in a blister pack and is suitable for filling small cracks. If the woods to be filled are to be varnished or stained, test prior to use, and mix with a quantity of stain if needed.

Paints

The paints that the average modelmaker uses will not generally be needed in large amounts. You should aim to build up a stock of colours in small tins, both of gloss and matt, of good quality enamels.

The comprehensive range of colours produced by Humbrol Paints satisfies all the modelmaker's requirements. Provided that the tins are sealed tightly after use, the colours will remain true, and of the correct consistency. It should not be necessary to thin the paints and all colours are intermixable. Excellent covering power, smooth finish and a quick drying time are the main requirements of the modelmaker. Humbrol Paints achieve these requirements, and their use is recommended.

No enamel will give an adequate cover on wood using a single coat because it is so porous. Some form of sealant will be necessary before a gloss finish can be applied. A single coat of either matt or gloss varnish, rubbed smooth when dry, will provide an adequate undercoat.

The use of 'wet-&-dry' rubbing paper is recommended throughout the building of the model, except upon those areas where a 'key' for glueing is needed. Fine quality sand- or glasspaper is ideal for these areas.

The thinning of paints and varnishes should not be necessary, using the modern compositions. If it does become necessary, or should you need to remove a spillage or stain, either white spirit or turpentine substitute may be used, in small quantities. Experience has given me a preference for white spirit; the lack

of oil within the liquid does not affect the properties of paint or varnish. **Avoid** completely the use of water-based paints, such as emulsion, for model work. These will invariably crack, or shrink, at a later date, spoiling the appearance of the model.

All paint work can be completed using brushes, unless the modelmaker is proficient in the use of, and has access to, an air brush. A comprehensive range of brushes is available, and you should try to acquire a stock of various sizes, and textures. If thoroughly cleaned after use, a good quality brush will last indefinitely, with little or no loss of hair. Cheaper brushes can shed hairs during use, and will spoil the finish of a model.

Varnishes
The foregoing remarks regarding quantities

A selection of paints.

also apply to varnishes. Small tins, or smaller tinlets, of a good quality matt or gloss polyurethane varnish, will be adequate for both working and display models.

Unlike the enamels, more than one coat is needed to provide an adequate finish, each coat being rubbed down after drying. With each successive coat, the grain of the wood will be more pronounced, and highlighted. Allow **at least** 24 hours between coats, leaving the subject in a dry, dust-free room if possible. Such patience will be more than adequately rewarded by the finish achieved.

The Humbrol range of varnishes are available in tinlets, tins and in the form of mini-sprays, similar to the paints.

Shellacs

Shellac is similar to varnish in appearance, but has a much shorter drying time – usually the part may be handled within an hour. The finish is much more 'subdued' than gloss varnish, having a slightly 'eggshell' appearance. Being of thinner consistency than varnish, care must be taken not to apply too much shellac, as runs and 'curtains' could occur.

French polish

Though similar to shellac in appearance, french polish is harder to apply correctly. It is best applied with a pad or sponge, and its fairly long drying time, coupled with little, or no, 'filling-in' properties between small cracks, reduces its value for modelmaking.

The choice of varnish, shellac or french polish, is, of course, yours. Any combination may be used with varying effect. For instance, the hull may be finished in a gloss varnish; the deck equipment in matt, the masts in shellac, etc.

Stains

If you wish to alter the colour of your model, you may either use a pre-stained varnish, or more usually, stain the piece prior to varnishing. Experience has shown that a water-based stain offers a greater latitude for depth of colour, than does a varnish-type stain. By using one, or more, coats of stain, you can control the depth of colour required.

The key to success in staining is to experiment on scrap wood **before** attempting the model. Alternatively, construct a card, using a small sample of **all** the woods in the kit. Using different varnishes, etc, coat one half of the wood with one coat, and the other side with two, or more. Note the differences. Repeat the experiment, using stains first.

By using a card, you can match the colour to the part, and gain knowledge of quantities to use upon the model proper. The graining within the woods will be seen to alter according to the angle from which they are viewed; this prior knowledge will help you to form a clear picture of the final appearance of your model.

Chapter 4: Building the Hull. First stages

Preparation

The largest single part of any model is the hull. Upon its construction and shape will depend the final model's appearance. **Do not** attempt to rush this, or indeed any, stage. Allow adequate drying time for the glue to set and harden. Use any means possible to provide a firm basis for the glue to work correctly. Rubber bands, clothes pegs, wire, thread, etc, will allow the parts to be held where conventional clamps will be ineffective, due to the curves involved. These are **all** methods which have been tried and tested over the years, and they all work.

A method of working which, to a large extent, leaves both hands free to work, should be aimed for. Experiment to find the easiest way to suit you, the modelmaker; the method described for a particular section may be difficult for you to handle, as described, but easy for another modelmaker. Additionally, a **left**-handed person will not work the same ways as a **right**-handed one.

It is recommended that the working base board, described in Chapter 11, is made before any construction is undertaken. The small cutting board should be also made, and used, from the start of building. Establish a

Using the working base board as a stand during the early stages of construction.

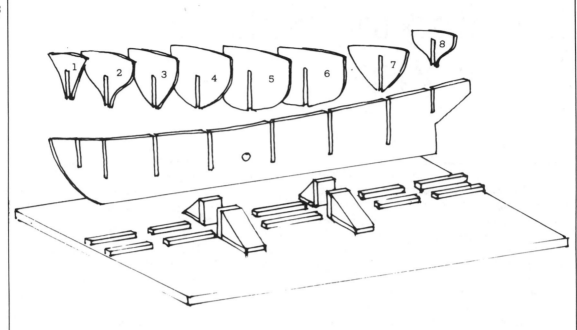

Keel and frames numbered 0-8 for clarity. The slots in the working base board allow the frames to fit between, thus reducing the distortion of the keel.

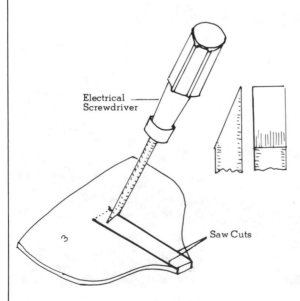

Electrical Screwdriver

Saw Cuts

The use of a sharpened screwdriver.

routine of identifying all the parts required for a particular section, and at all stages of that section, keep the parts together. Allow as much room as possible when working, and always replace unwanted items for that section back into the box lid to avoid loss.

Within the chapters the sequence of work for any section is provided by both drawings and photographs, for clarity.

First Stages

Identify all the parts required for the construction of the hull skeleton. These will be the false keel, frames (or formers), possibly some deck stringers (or strengthening pieces), and various shaped support blocks. The majority of kits number the parts for clarity, starting at Number 0 for the keel, and going up to 10 or 12 for the frames. Refer to the kit plans and instructions for exact number sequence.

Some slight trimming of the keel and frame slots may be needed to allow the parts to fit together, without strain or slackness. Fit the parts together until the join is satisfactory, **without glueing**. Work through all the frames

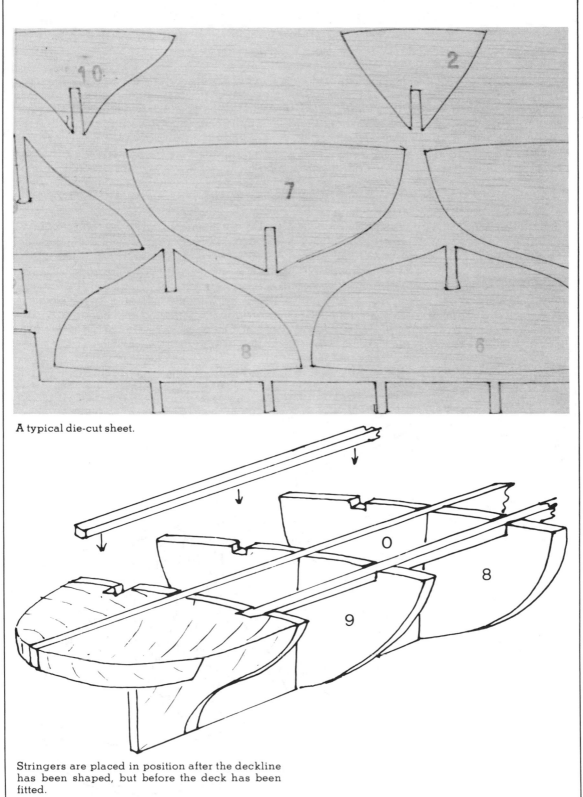

A typical die-cut sheet.

Stringers are placed in position after the deckline has been shaped, but before the deck has been fitted.

until all the parts fit, and then remove each frame. (This procedure is known as 'dry-fitting', and will be referred to throughout the construction of the model). Each frame **must** fit at 90 degrees to the keel, and be in a vertical position, when viewed from the side.

Refer to the drawing for the position of the 'stringers' (if used in the kit). Any additional slots and trimming for the stringers should be completed before glueing the frames into position.

Commencing at the front or bow, apply the glue into the slots provided, and, working carefully, place each frame into position. Once all the frames are positioned, place the assembly into the working base board, check that each frame is correct, and leave the whole assembly to dry completely, before attempting to start any other work.

Check to make sure no glue has touched the board – this will present difficulties later. Any normal adhesive glue excess may be wiped

away using a damp, **not wet**, cloth, before the glue starts to 'cure'.

Die-cut sheets

The term 'die-cut' simply means that the outline of parts is either impressed or drawn upon the sheet of plywood, or similar, and the parts need to be cut to shape. It **does not** mean that the parts may be broken, or forced from the outline! If this is attempted, some damage may occur. **Do** use either a small saw, or a very sharp modelling knife (refer to the Tool List in Chapter 11).

Do not attempt to cut all the complex curves needed in one operation. Cut out a series of blocks, or rough forms, and trim the curves later. Care is obviously needed, but the operation is simple. Slots can be cut out precisely with the aid of a small electrical screwdriver, sharpened and 'honed' to act as a chisel. Once the parts are cut out, proceed as before to assemble the skeleton.

Solid hull models

Solid hull models require very little work

The use of stern blocks.

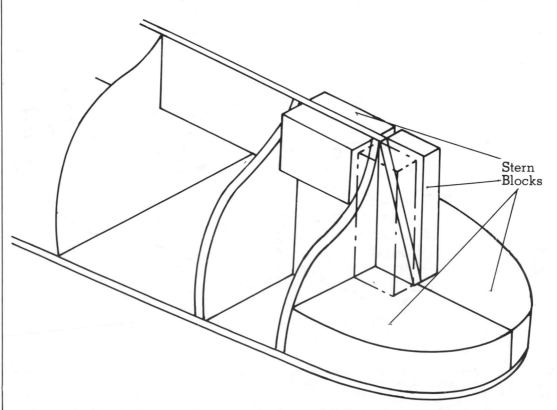

Stern Blocks

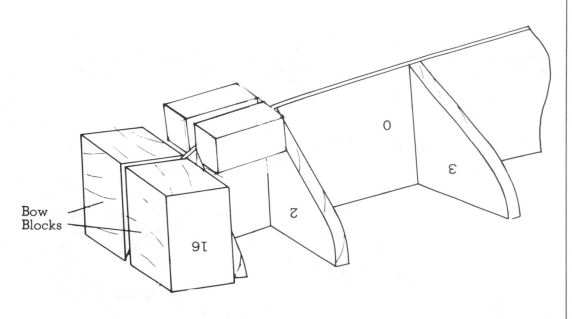

Bow
Blocks

The use of bow blocks.

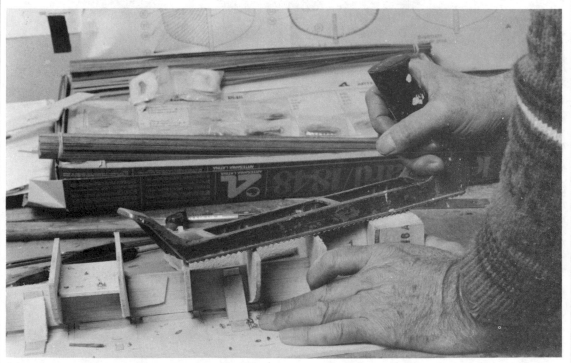

Smoothing the tops of the blocks and frames with a
surform.

Checking the deck line with the aid of a single plank.

Sanding the tops of the blocks and frames.

during the initial stages, and are therefore an ideal type of model for beginners. The hull is usually cut to a high degree of shape, and usually only needs sanding to remove any rough sections, before planking can commence (see Chapter 5 for information). Some marking to establish the positions of the various parts such as the keel, stem and sternpost may be needed, and you should refer to the kit instructions for guidance.

The necessary information will be found under the relevant chapters (ie planking, deck planking, rigging, etc). The same methods apply for both plank-on-frame models and solid hull models, once the initial hull has been completed, but where special instruction is needed for solid hull work, this will be included.

The support blocks

The position of the support blocks are shown in the drawings. The blocks should be allowed to protrude **above** the deck line slightly, and all the blocks are best placed into position in one

operation. Either Superstick or carpenter's adhesive may be used, the parts being held in position using some form of clamping, as before.

As the hull depends upon a firm, stable and strong structure, for future work, it is important that the blocks be given sufficient drying time – at least 12 hours. You can use this drying time to familiarise yourself with the next stages, or with the construction of some of the smaller parts. By working to this method, you will find that the necessary 'delay' is not such a hindrance. The concentration is transferred to the stage being worked, with the same results.

After the deck line of the frames and blocks has been trimmed to shape, as shown, the preparation of the false deck is undertaken. As this will obviously have to follow the curves across the tops of the frames, as well as the lengthways curve, it may be found that the panel provided requires a quite substantial force to make it bend to shape. This would put too much strain on the securing pins, and the distortion of the panel, whilst drying, may also

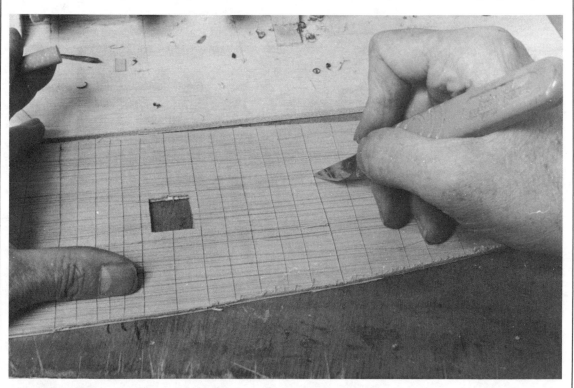

Scoring the underside of the false deck.

result in a gross shape. To eliminate this danger, score the underside of the panel with a sharp knife, or dart head, to a depth of approximately the width of one of the layers of plywood. This should be done both lengthways and crossways.

Dry-fit to the frames, testing both curves. **Do not** use too much force during dry-fitting, as the panel may crack. Continue to score until the panel will follow the curves correctly, touching both the centre keel and the edges of each frame. During this time, mark, on the top side of the deck, the centreline from bow to stern, and the position of each frame across the wood. This will help to establish the position of the pins, when being placed.

Using carpenter's wood glue, glue each frame and site where the deck will touch. Pin the deck into position, pinning along the length of the keel first to establish the most difficult curve. Remove the assembly from the working base board to pin the edges of the deck at approximately 2.5cm in from the edge.

Check to ensure that the deck panel does touch each frame at the edge. Hold the deck in position, using large rubber bands or lengths of wire wrapped tightly around the hull framework to ensure the tension is maintained whilst the glue is setting. Again, a quite long setting time is essential for this operation, and no further work should be attempted until the assembly has set.

Shaping the blocks and frames

The photographs and drawings should provide the necessary information for the typical methods of shaping the frames and blocks below the deck line. The reason for the long drying times should now become apparent, and it will be appreciated just how strong the structure has become. This, in turn, should give you confidence to use what may seem quite brutal tools to effect the needed curves.

As the planking will need to follow the curves produced, it is important that the maximum possible 'seating' is provided. The edges of the frames need to be shaped,

Glueing the frames where the deck will touch.

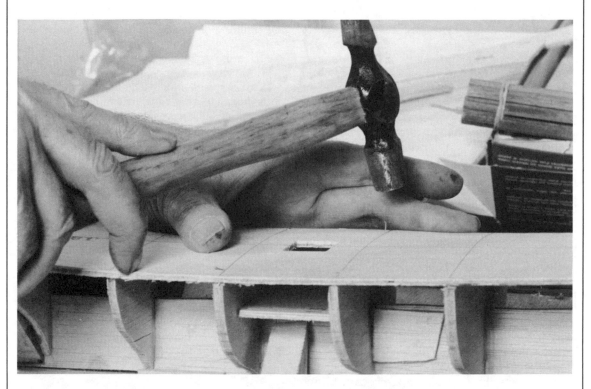

Pinning the deck to the frames.

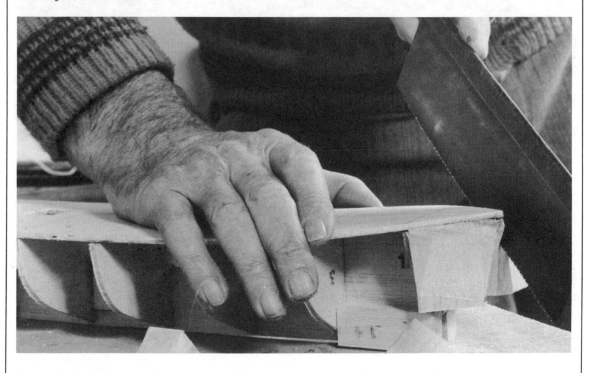

Sawing the bow blocks to shape.

particularly at the bows and stern, to provide this seating.

A point worth remembering is that the lines on a ship have to provide a smooth, clear profile to the water. There are no 'bumps' or depressions to spoil this profile, and the model should be the same. Therefore, when shaping or sanding, use as long a tool as possible. A long rasp-type file, a surform, a long sanding block, etc, will all ensure that the area being shaped will match the next area. Use a single plank from the kit, as shown, to check this continuity of line, and keep sanding and checking until satisfied.

Hints on construction

During construction, especially when planning the deck fittings, pre-shaping the waterways, etc, the use of a deck-shaped template will prove invaluable. This is best made while the deck line is clear and uncluttered. Any semi-stiff card will do; simply place the card on the table, with the model upside-down, and draw around the outline. Cut out the shape, and mark the card on the **opposite** side to the one drawn upon as the top.

To transfer accurately the outlines of the various fittings on the plans, simply trace them using a soft pencil. Turn the tracing paper upside down, and re-mark on the template. A faint outline will result, enough to re-draw accurately. Thus the position and shape of the fitting can be checked without using the actual hull; this will avoid marking deck planking, etc.

If, during the shaping of the frames and blocks, an accident occurs, causing the keel to crack, do not despair; simply use any scrap material to glue across the crack, using the same glue as before, and 'butting' the two sides together. Make sure any such join will be clear of the planking run, especially at the keel. Such a repair is seen in the photograph on page 21, near the No 6 frame on the model. It was needed because the false keel was cracked by someone stepping on it!

Smoothing the bowblocks with a surform.

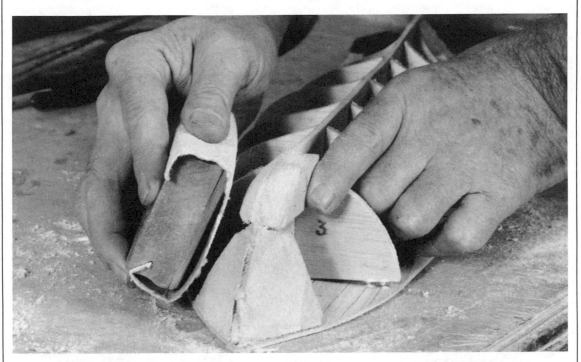

Sanding the bow blocks.

Checking the line of the frames with the aid of a
single plank.

Note the run of the bow planking.

Chapter 5: Planking the hull

Preparation

You will have noticed when checking the hull lines with the single plank that some degree of twisting and shaping will be needed to allow the planking to follow the shape. If you rely solely on the pins to hold the planking to the frames, some stress will occur, with the possible danger of the planking splitting, especially at the ends. Pre-shaping the plank to the shape required will eliminate this danger, and some methods, easily accomplished using simple equipment, are described below.

Steaming

Refer to the photograph on page 34. It will be seen that quite a dramatic shape can be achieved using an ordinary steam iron. As some degree of discoloration from the wood may result, use the working board to effect the bends. Place the board onto either an ironing board or a flat formica-type table top. Allow the iron to reach full working temperature, having filled it with water. Allow steam to pass over the plank for a few seconds, **before** attempting to bend it. Lift the end of the plank slowly and, without stress, gently upwards, moving the iron along the length of the plank, at the same time. Obviously you will need to experiment to gain expertise, and, to this end, I suggest that a single plank be used to attempt more and more complex shapes, until you are confident

Bending the plank after soaking.

Working/Cutting Board

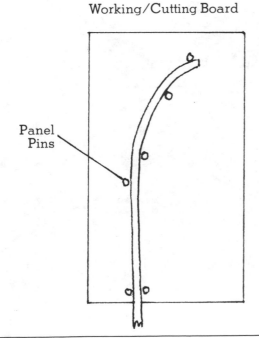

Panel Pins

Gentle Curve

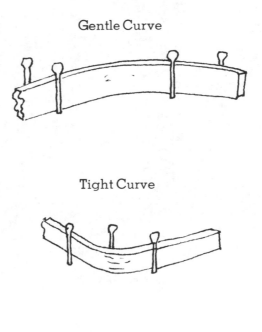

Tight Curve

of shaping to the required curve. You will also find that a quite dramatic degree of twisting of the plank can be reached, by simply forcing gently whilst the wood is affected by the steam.

The method sounds very complicated, but, as you will quickly find is really very simple and easy, once your initial nervousness has been overcome, and has the added advantage of the wood drying immediately, due to the heat, which means it can be glued and pinned at once. Use either cascamite or carpenter's wood glue. This method of pre-shaping is, in my experience, the most effective method of shaping, and can be used with confidence.

Soaking and Shaping

The same degree of shaping can be achieved quite simply by soaking a number of planks in a bowl or bath of hot water. The plank will soften and allow quite a high degree of bend and twist before splintering occurs. The plank, once soaked, can be either pinned directly onto the frames of the model, applying pressure to make the plank follow the line, or pre-shaped using a board. Pins are inserted into the board along the line required, and

marked. The plank is then made to follow the line and allowed to dry. The shape assumed will stay in the wood and will reduce the stress. The danger of this method is the possibility of the wood warping and assuming a different twist than the one intended. As this usually occurs later, quite a long drying time is really necessary. The main disadvantage is that you will not achieve the same holding effect from the glue, the plank mainly relying on the pins.

Indirect heat

This method is similar to the steaming method, without using steam. Basically it involves using some form of heat, such as a ordinary iron, or a tool such as a soldering iron. In both cases the main disadvantage is the possibility of marking the wood. The resin within the wood may overheat, causing the graining effect to darken. Similarly, too much heat will cause charring which will make the wood brittle, increasing the danger of splitting, when pinning.

The use of a soldering iron can be advantageous when the size of the wood is small, and very tight curves are needed. The

Bending planks using a steam iron.

key to the operation is not to allow the wood to remain on the heat but rather to gently move the piece, at the same time forcing the curve required.

As before, you should practice using scrap wood, until the method becomes apparent. It will be found, as with all these methods, that their application is very simple.

Green-stick fractures

As the model will contain very small parts, usually constructed from very thin woods, such as veneer, where the use of heat in any form is not practical, the 'green-stick' method can be used.

By holding the wood tightly with one hand and carefully forcing the curve with the other, a slight 'give' will be felt. Move the position of your hands slightly, and repeat. By 'breaking' at intervals of approximately 5mm, a gentle curve will be assumed. It must be stressed that **at no time** is the wood actually broken completely, hence the name of 'green-stick'.

The weakening of the wood will be repaired once the glue (cascamite or Superstick contact glue) has been applied, and any slight splintering which may occur on the outside of the curve should be left until the wood is in position before attempting to smooth. This method will be found to be particularly useful when fitting the rubbing bars around the rounded type of stern. As before, practise until proficient.

Veneers may also be curved by simply rubbing a thumb nail along the wood on the inside. The heat generated by doing this is quite adequate for the wood to bend.

Pinning the Planks

With the exception of solid hull-type models, the majority of kits rely on the planks being fastened to the frames by glue and pins. A systematic approach to this work is desirable, and should be practised until you are fully confident to work on the actual hull, as any mistakes will spoil the finished appearance.

The smallness of the pins, and their comparative 'softness', could result in more bent pins than straight ones, unless both a delicate and firm approach is employed. A pair of long-nosed pliers and a small, light hammer, such as a toffee hammer, should be

Bending a bulwark section using a steam iron.

employed. Refer to the drawings and photographs for guidance. Remember that the pin is soft, and do not attempt to drive in the pin completely with one stroke! A gentle, but firm stroke will gradually insert the pin, and the pliers will ensure that it does not bend.

The head of the pin should be cut off at a depth of approximately 3mm for appearance. This will also ensure that, when sanding, a total, smooth line around each pin head is achieved, rather than the sanding paper making small barely noticeable pockets around each pin, due to the pin head being proud of the wood.

Always apply glue (carpenter's wood glue or cascamite) to the full 'run' of the plank to be pinned **before** pinning. Always commence at the centre and work toward each end, holding the plank against the previous plank in position. Due to the curvature of the frames, it will be found that a plank may not follow the line of the previous plank, especially toward the bow or stern. **Do not** force the plank to adopt an unnatural line, as these gaps may be filled by the use of 'inserts' from wood of the same sheds, fashioned from the scrap produced when planking. **Do not** attempt to

place pins at the very ends of the planks, as splitting will almost certainly take place. Allow at least a 25mm overlap of each plank at both ends, and **do not** trim further until the glue of the planks has set completely.

Planking the hull

Some kits advocate commencing the planking from the deck line, others from the keel, upwards. The normal boatbuilding practice was to use the 'keel upwards' method, both for strength and to avoid distortion. The planks also adopted a more natural line when viewed from the bow or stern.

Until approximately five or six planks, on each side, have been placed, fit one plank on each side alternatively. If you 'sight' along the keel after fitting the first plank, you will see a quite obvious bend in the keel! This will disappear with the fitting of the first, other side plank, and should not create too much concern. The methods shown in the drawings and photographs will aid you.

There will come a point when it will be found that it is impossible to follow the lines of the

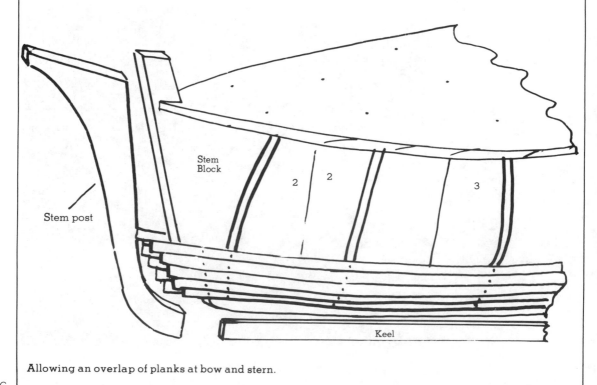

Allowing an overlap of planks at bow and stern.

A method of pinning the planks, using pliers as an aid.

Pinning planks to the hull. Note the glue on the frames.

Removing the heads of the pins.

View of the partially-planked hull.

previous plank, even with quite dramatic steaming. At this point, a shaped, half length, plank may be fitted. This is called a 'stealer'. The plank should be cut to approximate shape, dry-fitted to the hull, and gently steamed at both ends to allow it to sit closely, and to prevent the ends sticking out, with possible resultant damage. Refer to photographs.

If, during the planking, a frame top which protrudes above the deck line (as is the case with some kits) happens to get broken, do not glue it back into the position. Carefully mark the exact position and keep the fragment safe. Once all the hull and deck planks have been fitted, this part can then be replaced.

As mentioned before, **do not** trim (closer to the hull than 5mm) the surplus ends of the planks. Other parts, such as the stempost and rudder post, will need to be fitted at a later stage, into the gap created by the two sides of planking. Refer to photographs.

Shape, glue and pin all the planks into position, until the level of the deck is reached. Using a junior saw, roughly trim along the deck line any planks that protrude above the deck. Fit all the inserts required, using the techniques shown in the drawings and photographs. Allow the hull glues to set completely, and roughly sand the planked hull. Any small gaps still apparent may be filled using a wood filler, preferably water-based, as near to the shade of the wood as possible. Alternatively, using a scrap piece of planking, and a fairly rough piece of 'wet-&-dry' paper, collect the dust of the wood, mix with the glue used to plank the hull, and thin with a small amount of water. Work into any cracks, and allow to dry. This will ensure the shade is correct, and the cracks as a result impossible to detect. Plastic wood may also be used, mixing with stain to match the shade of wood.

'Stealer' plank.

STEALER PLANK.

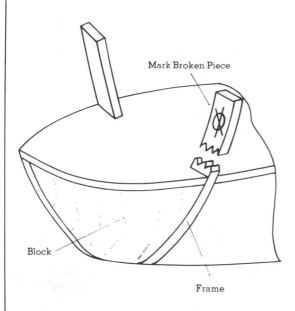

Mark Broken Piece

Block

Frame

Broken frame top.

Refer to the photographs and drawings for guidance for the next stage.

The gaps between the sides of the hull planks will need to be trimmed to allow the stem- and rudder posts to be fitted. Place the hull upside-down, as shown, and using a junior saw, very carefully saw **inwards** to create a gap the same thickness as the false keel. Identify both the stem- and rudder posts and adjust the gap to ensure a tight fit, without strain. **Do not** fit the parts at this stage.

Further trimming of the hull planks is now necessary for the fitting of the side rails, called 'bulwarks'. These are normally included in a kit as a long, shaped length of the same material as the false deck. This may vary from kit to kit, and may have all the various sections, such as cannon ports, access doors and wash port openings, already cut out. Refer to the kit plans for guidance, and trim the part if needed.

If a bulwark strip is included, the planking

Bow planks after initial trimming.

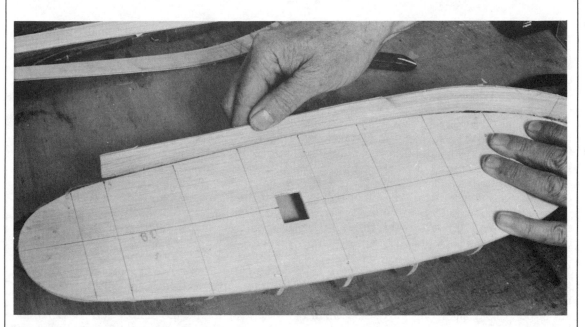

Dry-fitting the bulwark to the hull.

Marking the deck plank edges using paint.

will need to be cut to the level of the false deck, as shown. Mark the planks to a depth of approximately 3mm, a line which will follow the bottom edge of the false deck, throughout its length from bow to stern. Very carefully, using a sharp cutting knife, score the line drawn. A small tenon saw, or a junior saw, will thus have a 'key' to follow, and should prevent the saw slipping and marking the planking. **Do not** try to hurry this operation, and continue to cut gradually until the strip can be removed without splintering the other planks.

Dry-fit the bulwark strip and trim the planks until the correct line is achieved. The bulwark strip may be steamed to shape for easier fitting, and the end panels, which cover the stern, the 'transom', may also be dry-fitted to fit. If the stern is round, as with the model shown, the transom may be steamed, as before. **Do not** fit either part into position until the deck planking has been laid.

If, similar to the model shown, an additional deck panel is needed, this should be fitted and shaped, ensuring that the outside edges follow the previously fitted deck. Any additional deck pieces may be pinned into position after glueing, and allowed to dry. Refer to the kit plans for guidance.

Planking the Decks

Preparation

You must decide whether to lay the planks to scale, as referred to in Chapter 2, or to use the planks as provided. The planks may be laid straight from the kit, but for added realism, some additional work can be done. On full-sized vessels the planks needed to be waterproofed against the weather, and once the planks were laid into position on the decks, the gaps between the planks were sealed by a method called 'caulking'. This involved forcing 'oakum', a rough fibre, between the gaps. This was then given an overlay of hot pitch, or tar. Once the tar had set, the residue was removed, leaving a thin black line showing between the planks. To simulate this effect on a model is very simple, and various methods can be employed.

Edgeing

All the deck planks required should be gathered and held so all the edges are at the top. These may be held in a vice, if available, or, more simply, held tightly in one hand.

Using a black waterproof fibre-tip pen, carefully mark one edge of each plank, as shown. Test the pen **before** use on a scrap piece of planking, to satisfy yourself that the colour does not 'weep' through the grain and dries instantly. Each plank should have a black line on one edge only!

The same effect can be achieved using matt black paint, by applying it to the edges using a 'pad' made up from a soft piece of material. Great care must be employed not to apply too much paint at any one time. To this end, after dipping in the paint tin, press the pad lightly onto a scrap of card, to remove any excess, **before** applying as before. This method, if used, means that care must be employed when separating the planks, and it is better to let the planks dry completely before this is done.

Once dry, the planks should be cut carefully into equal lengths, as suggested on the plans and in Chapter 2. It is important that the ends of the planks are square to ensure accurate fitting on the decks, and to ensure the ends of the planks appear opposite each other. One end of the planks should also be marked as described, to simulate the butt joint of each plank.

Another method of 'caulking' is to lay the planks straight onto the deck after first smoothing with a fine paper. A gap between each plank is left during the laying, and into this gap a length of black cotton is laid. This method can be very messy, and does restrict the builder in the final smoothing of the deck planks, but may be attempted, if desired.

Laying the Planks

It is very important, for the sake of appearance, that the deck lines should be straight, with **no** bends in the lines of the planks. If not already drawn, mark the centreline of the model from the bows to the stern. Make sure all fixing pins are flush to the deck, and that the deck is slightly roughed with paper, to provide a 'key' for the glue.

Using the centreline as a guide, commence the planking by laying the centre plank through its full length. Lay each plank with the

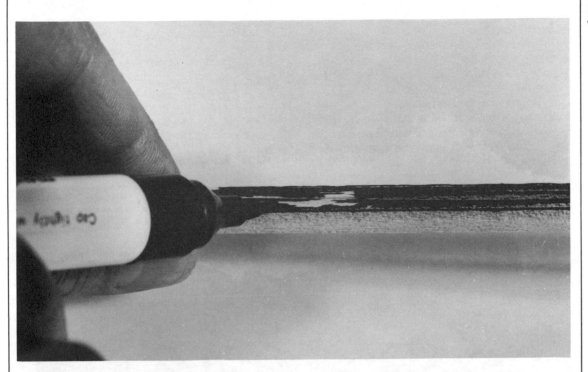

Marking the deck plank edges using a fibre-tip pen.

Sections of the deck cut out for deck fittings. Note
mitre joints.

painted edges facing the same way, and allow the planks to overlap the edges of the deck to be trimmed later.

Only plank one side of the deck at a time, and press each plank into position firmly against the preceding one, checking for straightness. Refer to both the plan drawings and to Chapter 2 for the position of each end of the planking. Note that no plank will have its end opposite the preceding one, and that an interval of 4 or 5 planks occurs before this happens.

Cover the false deck with cascamite or carpenter's glue, and spread evenly. Any surplus glue protruding from between the planks should be wiped away using a damp cloth. Press the planks firmly, both when laying and additionally after each section, to avoid any 'springing' of the plank, as the glue starts to dry.

Once the deck is planked completely, and the outside edges trimmed, refer to the kit plans for the position of the hatch openings, mast holes, etc. If it is intended to cut out the hatchways, etc, as suggested in Chapter 7, these should be carefully marked and the top planking cut out. Allow for any difference between the size as shown on the plans, and the actual building, by cutting slightly **smaller** than the actual size shown. This can be adjusted at a later stage, when the part has been constructed, and will also avoid splintering during sanding.

Once any additional work has been completed, sand the complete deck to a high degree of smoothness. Sand only in one

Deck planking complete with 'bolt' marks.

direction (from bow to stern), and remove any overlaps surrounding the deck edges.

The deck should now present an appearance as shown in the drawings, with a fine black line between each plank. The ends of the planks were fastened to the deck using bolts and dowel caps to match the wood. These may be simulated using the pins provided in the kit, but a much more effective and pleasing method is to simply mark them in, using a very fine, soft pencil, putting two marks at each end of the plank, as shown. The complete deck should now be given a single coat of Humbrol matt clear varnish and set aside to dry in a dust-free place, preferably with the model upside down.

The single coat will leave the deck with a dull appearance, simulating the actual decks, which were constantly scrubbed using 'holystones'.

Planking solid hull models

The planking on solid hull models is usually thinner than that on conventional 'plank-on-frame' models, and mainly consists of 'veneers' or similar material. This is applied quite easily using Superstick contact glue, applied to both surfaces, allowed to dry and pressed firmly into position. Because of its thinness, and consequent ease of cutting, any trimming of the plank shapes can be done quite easily once the plank is in its final position. A 'stealer' plank, for instance, may be laid without any prior trimming. Simply lay the plank, allowing the ends to overlap the preceeding one. Press very firmly, and by running either a fingernail, or the blunt end of a cutting knife, over the overlap, the edge to be cut to shape will become clear. Once cut, because of the contact glue, the shaped edge will fit correctly into position.

Deck planking

Various alternatives to the method described previously can be used, and any, or all, could be used, if the builder wishes.

Mark the planks directly onto the deck by means of a very fine, soft pencil, continuously sharpened to maintain the thin line. The use of a straight rule is very important, and great care must be taken to make sure that the lines are exactly the same distance apart. The same method, but using a wood gauge, to score the groove into the wood may also be used. After scoring, the deck should be very lightly rubbed down to a smooth finish, and, using a pad, rather than a brush, given a single coat of varnish, as before. This will darken the groove sufficiently to become apparent, and no further work, other than a light 'wet-&-dry' sanding, will be needed.

Yet another method, involving the use of a template previously cut out, may also be employed. The template, preferably cut from white, semi-glazed card, should be lightly stained using Humbrol clear polyurethane matt varnish. This will give the white card a slightly golden effect. Once this coating has dried completely, the deck planking markings may be scribed on the card, either in pencil, or 'scored' as before. A second coat of matt varnish, applied with a pad, will bring the deck to the required colour. When dry, this may be glued into position, using a contact glue. The advantage of this method is that **all** the marking can be done on a flat surface, thus ensuring greater accuracy.

A similar method involves the use of plasticard (thin sheets of plastic). The plastic should be rubbed down with a 'wet-&-dry' paper, using plenty of water, and rubbed in a fore and aft direction only. The marking is done precisely the same way, but using only a gauge to 'score' the sheet. Instead of a varnish, initially, use a water-based light oak stain, both prior to, and after, the scoring. The slight marking of the card ensures that a slight 'graining' effect will be noticed, which becomes even more prominent after a single coat of matt varnish is applied.

THE HUSSARD
circa: 1848

Note the internal and external bulwark detail.

Chapter 6: Fitting the Bulwarks, Stern and Stemposts etc

Fitting the bulwarks

The bulwarks, or side rails, should be identified, checked for shape, and trimmed to fit into the rebate provided, as described in Chapter 5. The fitting is quite simple, and the part is secured by pinning to the deck edge, after applying glue (cascamite or carpenter's glue) to all the surfaces required.

In the case of a 'square' stern, as shown, the join may be given an additional holding coat of glue, on the insides of the two parts. **Do not** trim any overlap until the glue has set completely. The parts may be held using rubber bands or pegs to aid positioning.

Allow to dry completely, as the further work entails some strain being placed upon the bulwarks, and a good tight fit is essential. Extra Bond glue should be used for this joint.

Fitting the stempost

The shaped stempost fits into the gap left by the two lines of hull planks, as described in Chapter 5. To aid the positioning, and to provide additional strength, after ensuring the accurate fit of the part, drill two small holes approximately 25mm apart down the length of the stem. Into these holes will be inserted two panel pins, of sufficient length to fasten into the internal false keel. The two holes drilled previously will ensure that the wood will not split during this operation, the Extra Bond glue providing additional strength.

Fitting the keel

The keel should be fitted in a similar way, also with two or more panel pins inserted, for strength. Additionally, two larger holes for the stand holding screws, described in Chapter 11, should be drilled. It is **very important** that the screw holes thus drilled are of adequate

size, and that screws intended for this purpose, should be tested in the holes **before** fitting the keel to the model. Cut out the angles needed very carefully, where the keel butts to the stem, as any gaps will be very noticeable on the completed hull.

Fitting the rudder post and rudder

The fitting of the rudder post differs slightly from the other external parts, as the rudder is attached to the rudder post **prior** to fitting to the hull, as described in Chapter 7. Therefore, the rudder post should be dry-fitted to ensure a very tight fit, and left to be fitted at a later stage. All angles between the keel and the rudder post should be cut and trimmed very carefully. It is recommended that the foregoing sequence be followed as described, to make the cutting of the various angles more simple. With the stem and keel in position, the planking of the bulwarks may now be completed, together with all ancillary parts.

It is recommended that, once the keel has been fitted, the stand, as described in Chapter 11, be used to provide support for the model **without** (at this stage) securing it to the hull.

Planking the bulwarks

In the model shown, the bulwark planks are of veneer. The fitting is as described in Chapter 5, for planking of solid hull models. The planking should be carried up to the level of the top of the bulwarks, and when dry, should be trimmed to follow the line of the top edge of the bulwarks. Along this line will be fitted the gunwale or rail top, when other ancillary parts have been fitted.

Should your model differ from this arrangement, such as continuing the hull planks up to the gunwale, or have only partial

47

bulwarks, the kit instructions will explain the method to be used. Some types of alternative fitting are illustrated as a guide.

Where the cannon ports are cut from the bulwarks, accurate measurement by studying the kit drawings is essential. The ports, or any opening, should be 'lined' using either the same material as the planks, or to give the model greater effect, from a contrasting shade. If the cannon ports have lids fitted, these are best cut from scrap material of the same thickness as the bulwarks, and lined with the planking before fitting into position.

In the model shown, doors at the bow and stern were fitted to allow the carronade (a large bore cannon) to be trained to any angle. For appearance's sake, the model doors were constructed from a contrasting material, and, to aid the curvature around the stern, the grain of the wood is vertical. This ensures that, when glued, the wood will follow completely the rounded curve without splitting or distortion. Superstick contact glue should be used throughout the foregoing operations.

Shaping the rubbing bars

The rubbing bars referred to served two purposes on smaller vessels. They provided

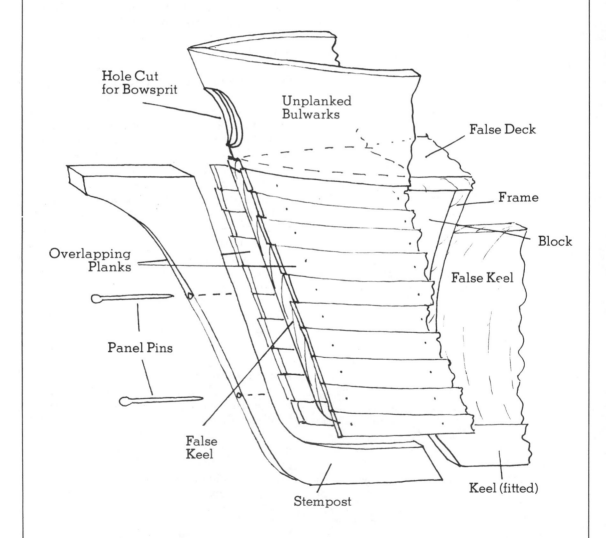

Dry-fitting the stempost. Note the larger panel pins.

additional strength to the vessel, and helped to avoid damage when coming alongside a quay or another vessel.

The rubbing bars should be pre-shaped as before, and dry-fitted into position. It may be found that the curvature around the rounded stern, as shown, is best accomplished with the aid of the soldering iron type of shaping, due to the very tight curves. Alternatively, the green-stick method may be employed (both described in Chapter 5). If both these methods fail, the builder may still follow the curvature by cutting small sections of the bar, glueing individually around the stern, filling any gaps

with wood filler or stopper, and sanding to shape when dry. Unless the latter method has had to be employed, **do not** fit the bars into position at this stage. The inner bulwark planking should also be fitted during this stage of work, in the same manner as described in the above, using Superstick contact glue.

Trimming the stem and stern planks

Before any other work is undertaken, the slightly protruding edges of the planks at the stem and stern posts should be carefully rubbed down, to provide a smooth join where the two parts meet. The line where the planks

The planks at the bow trimmed ready for dry-fitting the stempost.

Dry-fitting the stempost.

finish should be straight and follow the curve of the stempost down to where it meets the keel. Similarly, the keel planking should be smoothed to finish, and all the planking checked to ensure no gaps have occurred during the drying-out period. Refer to the drawings.

Sealing the hull

The complete hull should now be sanded to a smooth finish, wiping the dust from the model using a damp, clean cloth. Allow to dry, and coat the inside of the bulwarks with a single matt clear varnish coat. If you want the shade of the model to be different to that of the planking (see Chapter 3), the appropriate shade of wood dye should now be applied. Allow to dry and smooth using a very fine paper. The purpose of this coat of varnish is to reduce the possibility of staining in some way the smooth 'raw' wood. Small sticky hands, especially if covered in jam, can leave a lasting stain upon the model.

The bulwarks fitted, with the stempost dry-fitted in position.

The ancillary parts, such as the rubbing bars, stay platforms (or 'tables'), gunwales and stanchions (inner bulwark supports), all have to be glued to the wood, and the chance of the glue smearing on to the other woods is greatly increased. By providing the seal, this danger is virtually eliminated, as the residue can be wiped away much more easily.

After mixing the varnish well, using a soft brush, apply a single **thin** coat of varnish to the entire hull. It will be noticed that the varnish will almost all be soaked into the wood, leaving a very dull, unattractive finish. This is to be expected at this stage, and should not cause you any concern. When dry the complete hull should once more be smoothed, only this time using a fine 'wet-&-dry' paper and plenty of water. Some idea of the type of finish to be expected from the final coats of varnish, yet to be applied, will now be gained. The model will feel satin-like to the touch, and the minute cracks left by the planks will have started to disappear.

Assuming that the hull is now dry, the rubbing bars, previously shaped, can be fitted, using Superstick contact glue. Note the position on the kit drawings, and, using a soft pencil, carefully mark the position on the model. Note that the line does **not** follow the line of the gunwale but rather follows the deck line, at approximately the same level.

Fitting the rubbing bars

Before fitting, dry-fit once more to ensure the angle of the bar is correct and will continue from the stem to 'half round' the stern. The join of both bars should come exactly at the centre of the stern, in the case of the model shown. A square stern join is obviously much easier to fit, the cross rubbing bar being measured prior to the long side pieces being fitted, for ease of fitting. Allow some slight overlap to the side pieces of the stern, to provide an undetectable square join. Ideally this join should be of the mitre type, and if you feel confident, this type of join should be attempted.

View of the model, showing the bulwarks, stanchions, waterways, cut-outs on deck for the fittings, etc.

When the actual fitting commences, along the line marked upon the hull, carefully lay a thin line of contact glue. Care must be taken to use the minimum amount possible to avoid residue squeezing out. Apply the glue to the inside of the rubbing bar, and allow to touch-dry. Commencing at the bows, lightly place the bars into position, avoiding pressing until the true position has been established. Once satisfied, press firmly throughout the full length, noting any residue that has protruded and removing before it sets. Fit the other side in a similar manner and set aside to dry.

The appearance of the rubbing bars may be enhanced by placing pins into the length of the part, taking care that the pins will be above

the line of pins securing the hull planks. This is entirely your choice. Due to the thinness of the bulwarks, it is not advisable to continue the line of pins up to the gunwale, as the builder will not be able to use any form of force, such as a hammer, to place the pins. If however you want, pins may be inserted by drilling a hole at the site of each pin, cutting each pin to size (to the thickness of the bulwark), and inserting into the hole provided. Alternatively, the pins may be 'suggested', using a fine point fibre-tip pen or a fine soft pencil. Where one or more rubbing bars, or other shaping pieces are shown on the kit plans, the above method of fitting should be employed. It must be emphasised that the marking of the parts, prior

Fitting the stern carronade doors.

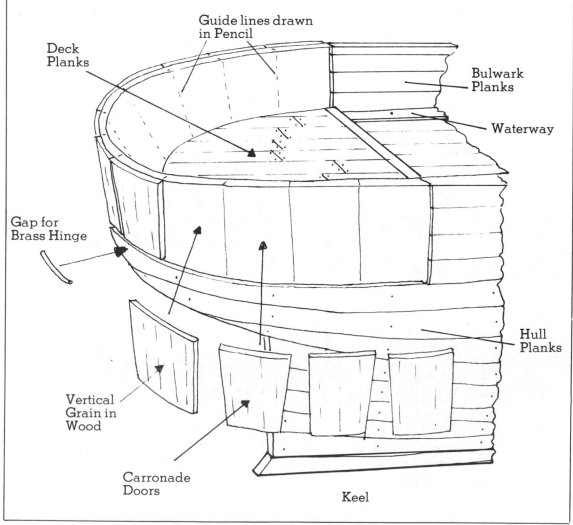

Guide lines drawn in Pencil

Deck Planks

Bulwark Planks

Waterway

Gap for Brass Hinge

Hull Planks

Vertical Grain in Wood

Carronade Doors

Keel

to fitting, is critical. **Both** sides **must** be equal in both depth and curvature, and to check the correctness, templates should be made at different lengths along the hull.

Fitting the waterways

Most kits usually have a waterway shown in the drawings. This is fitted above the planks and to the inner edge of the bulwarks. For the sake of appearance it is usually constructed of a different colour wood than the deck planking. The part should be pre-shaped, by steaming, using the deck template as a guide (Chapter 4), and using contact glue. Once in position the part may be pinned for effect, drilling the holes prior to fitting. As before, the

excess glue should be removed to prevent staining of the deck planks. Refer to the drawings for guidance.

Fitting the stanchions

The stanchions are fitted along the full length of the inner bulwark, and the base needs to be trimmed slightly to allow a smooth join. The angle of the join will alter from the bows, which will be quite pronounced, to the centre of the model, and increase once again nearer the stern. Because of this, it is recommended that each stanchion is cut and fitted individually. Although this appears, at first reading, to be very time-consuming, bear in mind that the deck fittings will be a focal point on the finished

The stern doors in position.

model, so any badly fitting join will be particularly noticeable. Similarly, the tops of each stanchion will provide a support for the gunwale, when fitted, and care must be taken to ensure that the top of each stanchion fits flush to the level of the rail top. It will be found that if the top does protrude over the level of the bulwark, it will present difficulty in removing the excess without causing damage.

Refer to the kit drawings for the spacing of each stanchion, and mark the position with a soft pencil. Make sure that the stanchions on both sides of the model are exactly opposite.

Fitting the pin rails
At intervals along the bulwarks pin rails are fitted on most models. These are quite simply platforms into which the belaying pins were held. A belaying pin was used to tie-off the ropes leading down from the rigging, and 'belay' means to stop, or hold. The method shown should clarify the way to tie-off the ropes (see Chapter 9). Remember when fitting the pin rails, to leave sufficient space between the gunwale, and between each pin, to allow the ropes to be coiled. Use carpenter's wood glue for all the above operations, carefully

removing any excess glue with a damp cloth.

The pin rails should be identified, shaped and drilled before fitting, and, as shown, usually fit on the top of a slightly shorter stanchion. Some pin rails are a complete assembly, which fits independently of the rails and stanchions, and so various types are shown.

Fitting additional rail pieces
In order to strengthen the vessel, additional inner bulwark support pieces were fitted, usually in the bows, where the strain was the greatest. These were fitted between each of the foremost stanchions, approximately mid-way between the deck level and the gunwale top. Refer to the kit plans for guidance, and the drawings for actual fitting methods. Note that any stanchions or deck fittings **must** leave enough room for the bowsprit to assume its position, and all fittings must be trimmed to shape.

Whilst the deck is still uncluttered, the position of the deck fittings such as eyebolts, cleats, 'bitts' (or bollards) should be noted and marked. The holes for the eyebolts should also be drilled, using a 1mm drill. Note the position

Internal cross-section, showing the deck plank markings, waterways, stanchions and the pre-drilled pin rail.

of any eyebolts which fit into the stanchions; to these will be fitted the gun carriage 'tackles', and these holes should also be drilled. The holes into which the masts will fit should also be drilled, if not done previously, using the centreline plank as a guide to ensure the masts will be in line with each other and the bowsprit.

Fitting the gunwale

The gunwale is usually fitted from one piece of wood, of a different shade to the hull planks. The part may be steamed to shape, using the bulwark top for guidance, and, if the rail is to be

pinned later, the holes for the pins should be drilled. By employing the prior drilling, the pins may be inserted with the minimum of force, thus reducing the possibility of damage.

Before attempting to fit the part, the bulwark top, to which the gunwale is fitted, should be shaped to achieve the correct curvature. It is important that the curve has no 'bumps' or 'dips' along its length, as this will spoil its appearance. To effect the curve, use a long sanding block with a medium paper to provide a good 'key' for the superstick glue.

If, because of the 'flat' shape of the gunwale

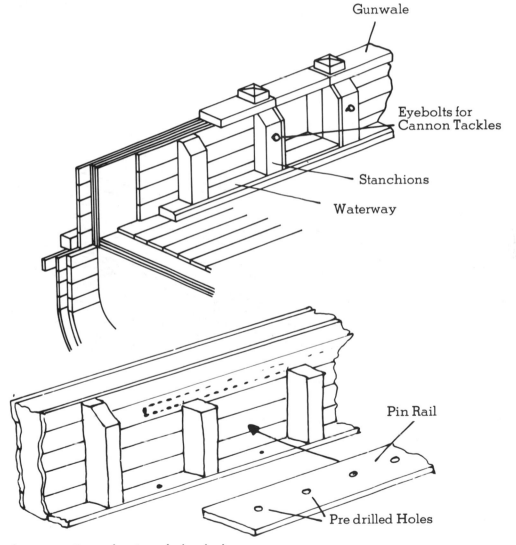

Internal cross-section, showing deck planks, waterways, stanchions and bulwarks.

to be fitted, you find that the curve of the stern cannot be achieved, the gunwale may be cut into small sections, as small as 5mm in length if necessary, and glued into position. The final curvature can thus be left until the glue is completely set, and the parts have gained strength. Remember to shape the curve of the **inner** gunwale as well as the outer! Refer to the drawings for guidance.

Fitting the shroud (or stay) supports

Where the rigging stays are fitted to the outside of the model, they need to provide a strong support. The stress of 'setting up' the rigging will place quite a substantial strain on these parts, and the join must be firm. Note the position and number of supports, called 'tables', on one side of the model. Mark carefully each position with a pencil, and check that each table is **exactly** opposite to the one on the other side.

Identify the wood recommended for tables, and carefully mark the size of each table. Lightly score each length to clearly define each part. Measure the distance apart that each deadeye (or rigging block) has to be on each separate table. Ensure that corresponding opposite tables are exactly the same, both in length and the position of the deadeye holes. This is important as once the

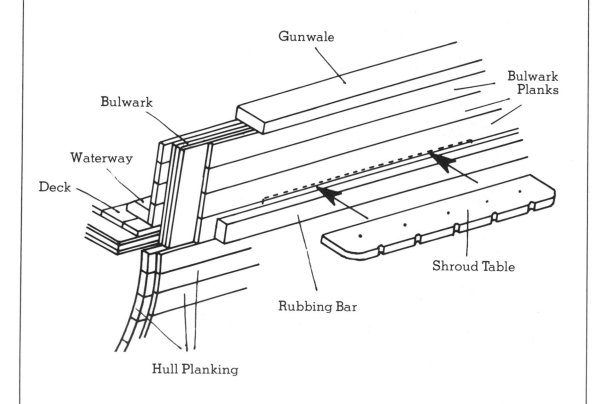

Typical **external cross-section**, showing rails, gunwale, bulwark planks, shroud table, etc.

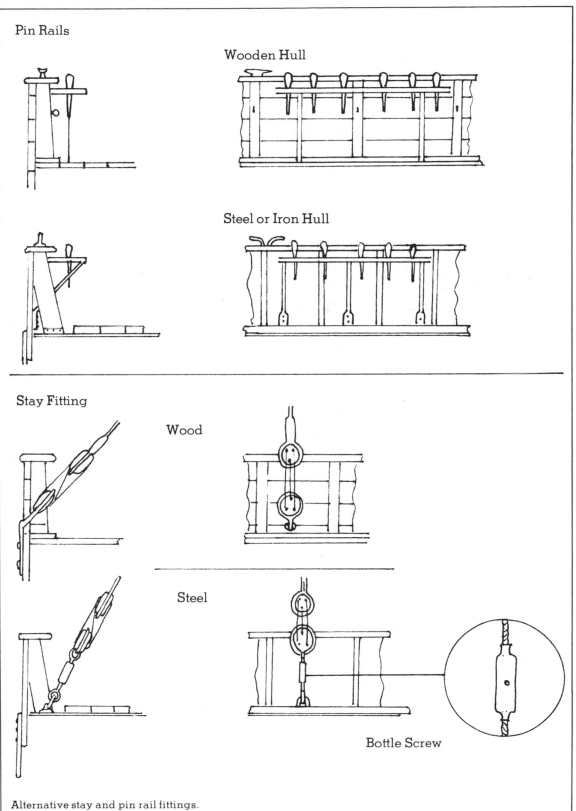

Pin Rails

Wooden Hull

Steel or Iron Hull

Stay Fitting

Wood

Steel

Bottle Screw

Alternative stay and pin rail fittings.

model has been rigged, the appearance may be spoilt if any variation is apparent.

Using a dart head, or suitable sharp point, impress a slight hole into the wood at the exact position of the pencil marks for each deadeye. This will ensure that the drill will produce the hole in the correct position. Drill all the holes needed along the uncut length of wood, and smooth the wood to a high **degree** of smoothness on both sides.

Using the mark previously scored, cut each table and place into pairs. The width of each table should be carefully noted, and, at the position required, already marked, cut out the layer of planking on the side of the bulwark. As the tables usually are seated along the upper rubbing bar, this additional rebate will provide a much stronger join. Additional strength to the join may be provided by placing an extra line of glue under the table where the bar and table meet; Extra Bond glue will provide additional strength, where required.

Repeat this process until all the tables are in position; the hull should then be set aside, using the stand, and allowed to set before any further work is attempted. The method of securing the table deadeyes is shown in the drawing and photographs, and should be completed at this stage. Once the tables are secure, fit a deadeye into each pre-drilled hole. Around each dead eye wind a length of wire, twisted tightly, leaving a 'tail' of approximately 50mm. Lightly insert a single pin directly under the pre-drilled hole, and wind the 'tail' around the pin. Apply a smear of Superstick contact or Superfast epoxy glue to the pin to aid security. Tap the pin completely into place, and leave to dry. Once it is completely dry, grasp the end of the 'tail', and wind in a circular motion until the wire near the pin snaps off. This may be either left bare or, preferably, painted with matt black. When varnished, the wire will assume the character of rope, giving a very neat effect. Refer to photographs for guidance.

Some models have internal rigging supports, some being fastened inside the bulwarks, and some others carry through the bulwarks and are fastened to the outside of the vessel.

Some types are shown, exploded for clarity, and reference to the kit plans and instructions should be made for guidance.

Chapter 7: Deck Fittings

Deck Fittings

The following is not in any particular fitting sequence, but merely for information.

The type and quality of the deck fittings will vary from kit to kit and the construction and fitting described in this chapter is intended to provide an informative cross-section of the various types. Similarly the position of the fittings may be different, and you will need to refer to the individual instructions for explanation.

All the fittings on the model should be fitted before the rigging of the masts are attempted. Consequently great care must be taken not to miss even a single eyebolt, or cleat, as, invariably, this will be the one absolutely necessary for fitting purposes, and **cannot** be fitted with the masts and rigging in place! A systematic approach is necessary to ensure this does not happen: all eyebolts should be fitted together; all cleats should be fitted together.

The purpose of each part, and the fitting, plus some exploded views, will be included

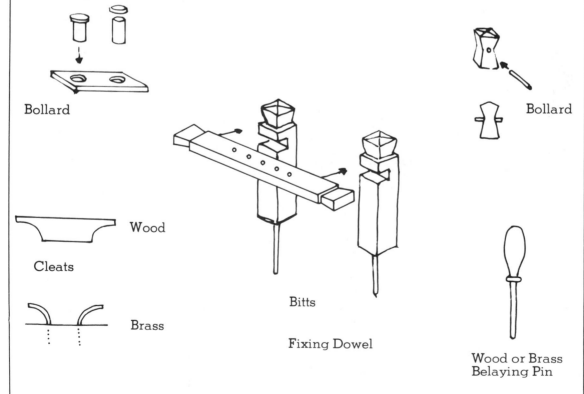

Bollard

Bollard

Cleats — Wood

Brass

Bitts

Fixing Dowel

Wood or Brass Belaying Pin

Exploded view of bitts, bollards and cleats.

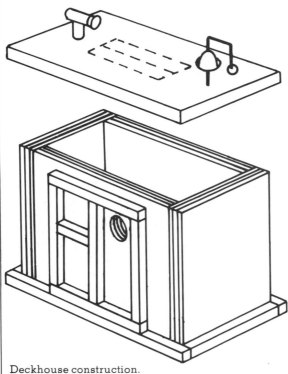

Deckhouse construction.

The finished deckhouse. Note the bell rope.

within this chapter, for guidance only. It is not intended as a definitive description of all the fittings to be found in any one kit, and this fact should be appreciated.

Normal adhesive, such as carpenter's wood glue or cascamite, will be adequate for the fitting of all the deck equipment, unless otherwise stated.

Bitts

Bitts or bollards are the means of securing the heavier types of ropes leading from the capstans, winches, windlasses, yards, etc. They are constructed quite simply, though it must be stressed, accuracy in the measurement is essential, as with all small fittings. Refer to the drawings showing construction; once the piece has been assembled, either lay it flat under a weight, or place it in a clamp, or vice, to eliminate any distortion.

To increase the strength of these parts when in position on the model, a small wood dowel, or pin, can be glued into a corresponding hole drilled into the deck in the correct position. This will avoid the part being displaced if knocked, and provide a means of tensioning the rigging. Complete the assembly by gently rubbing on a piece of fine sandpaper (laid flat) to remove any ridges, and use Extra Bond glue for security.

Deckhouses

The construction and shape of deckhouses differed with every ship, and some types are included, exploded for clarity. Each deckhouse should be completed, including varnishing or painting, before fitting to the deck.

Cabins and 'scuttles'

On smaller vessels large deckhouses were impractical, and the provision of light for the crew virtually unknown. Any light felt to be necessary was provided by small, usually round, pieces of glass let into the deck. The officers did not live in luxury either. Access to their cabins was usually by means of small deck fittings called 'companionways'.

To allow head room, the after end was usually higher than the forward end, with a small door to allow access to the ladder fitted

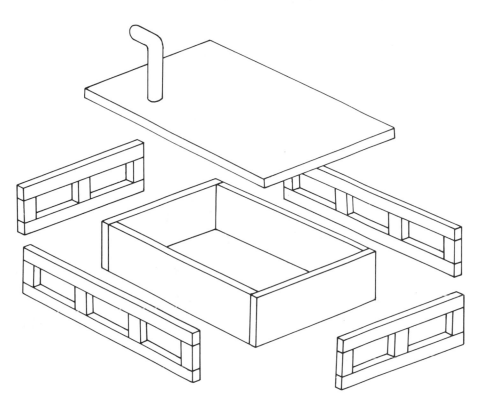

Smaller deckhouse construction.

within. These fittings may or may not have had port holes or scuttles fitted, and if the information given is hard to believe, it must be remembered that there was rarely more than 1.50m of headroom below decks – hence the custom on British naval vessels of drinking the Sovereign's health sitting down! Only when the vessel was considerably larger was adequate standing room provided.

Hatchways

The loading hatches are constructed very simply, and most parts are normally included within the kit. The various types are shown, and you may use any variation desired. The hatch could be shown open, with the associated hatch-board in close proximity, or shown with a cover in place. If an open type is preferred, a corresponding hole must be cut into the deck to aid appearance, and great care must be employed to cut accurately.

Winches and windlasses

Winches to aid the trimming of the sail yards etc, did not come into general use, especially on the smaller type of vessel, until the advent of the stately clipper ship. The tremendous leverage needed to trim the sail was found to be beyond the small crews, and gradually sail winches were developed. Some types are included in the drawings, and the construction is quite simple, provided care is employed.

Windlasses were used to pull the larger vessels anchors up to the deck line for securing. They were not found in the smaller vessels, which relied upon a capstan to do the work. A 200-ton vessel would have an anchor chain of c30m, which would need 8-10 men to haul it in. Typical examples are shown in the drawings, and these differed according to the period of building.

Tillers, steering gear and wheels

The smaller vessels were steered with a tiller. This was fitted to the top of the rudder where it came through the deck, and was moved in the opposite direction the vessel was required to go. Larger vessels fitted with a tiller would, of necessity, also be fitted with tackles to aid the helmsman.

Gradually the tiller was replaced by the steering wheel; at first this was no more than a

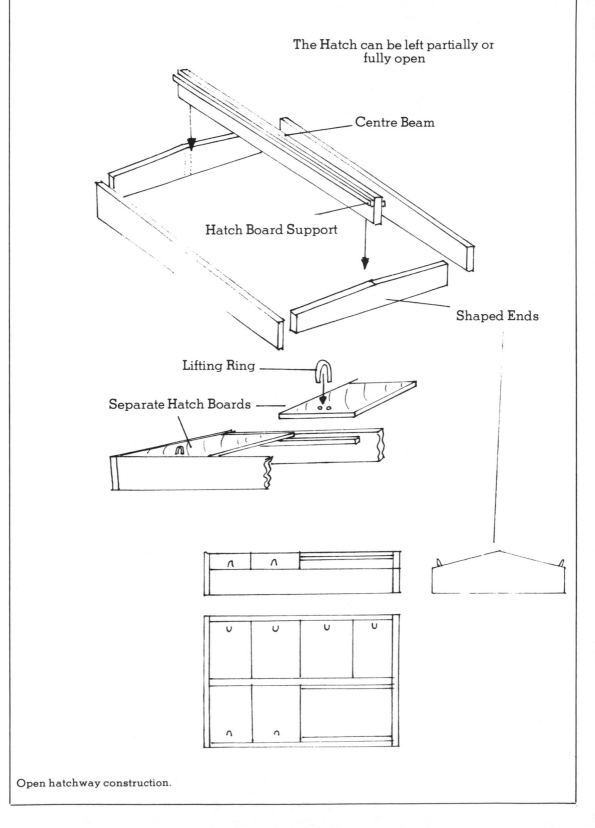

The Hatch can be left partially or fully open

Centre Beam

Hatch Board Support

Shaped Ends

Lifting Ring

Separate Hatch Boards

Open hatchway construction.

series of tackles, leading from the tiller, and terminating at a round 'barrel' attached to a wheel, to which the tackle ropes were attached. The type shown in the drawings is similar to those fitted to Captain Cook's **Endeavour** and **Resolution**.

Gratings

Most vessels had gratings. They were used to provide ventilation and light. During 'heavy' weather they could be covered by a tarpaulin, an oiled or tarred canvas cover. The ones included in the kits need to be assembled, and are usually included ready cut to size. They are assembled very simply, though care must be employed not to force the parts. **Do not** attempt to glue them together, but once completed, the base of the grating may be given a light smear of glue to hold the parts. Remove any residue between the holes with a very small point, such as a dart.

Ladders

The ladder included within the kits is usually pre-cut, and only needs glueing together. Additional extras such as hand rails or sides

may also be included, and the complete fixture assembled before fitting to the model. The types with rungs, rather than steps, may also be needed on some models, and the construction is shown.

Catheads

The name of this particular part stems from the practice of 'catting' (or securing) the head of the anchor, before lifting up the lower parts or 'flukes', for stowage purposes. This involved the position shown in the drawings, the reverse procedure being adopted when ready to use the anchor once more. One or more rope sheaves, or 'pulleys', were incorporated within the cathead, and a tackle rigged to pull up the deadweight of the anchor. You may show the anchors in any position, according to preference, and may show one anchor stowed with the other ready to drop.

Cannon and carronades

The drawings showing the construction of these parts are self-explanatory. The ancillary tackles and ropes, shown in the photographs, may be fitted if desired. The ring bolts are

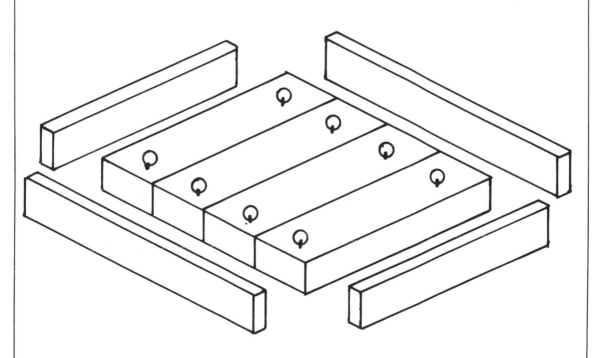

Typical kit hatchway.

Hatchway or scuttle made from scrap material and fixed to a perspex base.

secured into the carriage using a smear of Superfast epoxy glue, and the carriage fastened to the deck by glueing a small piece of wood under the base, to the depth of the wheels. By applying glue to this piece of wood, rather than the wheels, a much more secure bond is affected with the deck.

Anchors

Most anchors included within the kits are quite accurate in their scale and construction. Some are not made from materials which will bend without breaking, and extreme care must be taken to avoid undue strain, if attempting to correct a badly-shaped part. It will be noticed that the top, cross, member of the anchor, the stock, is at right angles to the lower (or flukes) part. This was to force the flukes to dig into the sea-bed to make the anchor grip. When placing the anchor in a position of temporary stowage on the model, the stock should be

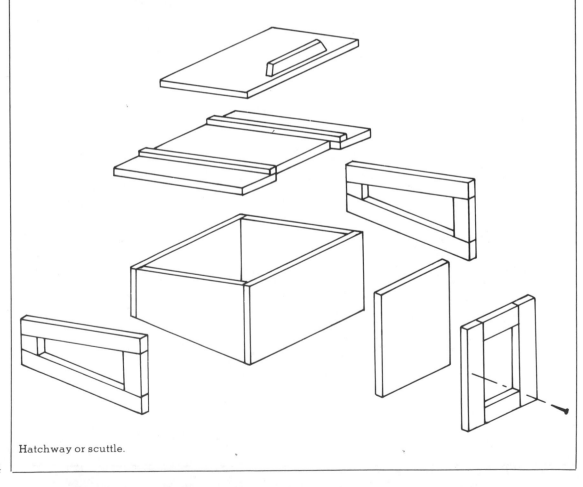

Hatchway or scuttle.

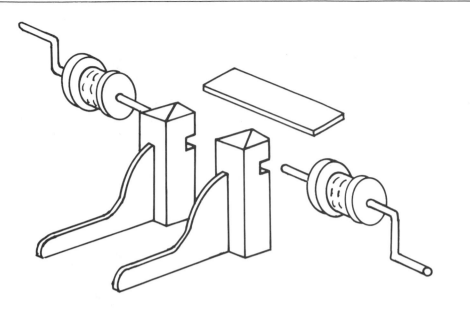

Sail winch, c1750.

The open hatchway, showing the capstan, foot bars
and deckhouse.

allowed to lie down along the hull sides, while the flukes should be hooked over the rail, and lashed into position.

Assembling the rudder

As mentioned during Chapter 6, the fitting of the rudder post and rudder, was best left until a later stage. The hinges, which allow the rudder to move freely, are fitted to both the post and the rudder. The actual position is shown in the drawings. Note that the rudder hinges are above the ones on the post.

Refer to the kit drawings and transfer the positions onto the parts. Identify from the kit,

the two, or more, sets of hinges, and, if not pre-drilled, drill using 1mm drill.

Transfer the position of these holes onto the parts and, using a dart point, carefully make a very slight hole. This is to allow the pins to enter with a minimum of effort. The number of pins required should be cut to length (just short of the width of the parts) and, working one side at a time, the pins should be lightly inserted, to almost the full length. Repeat on the opposite side, and by either placing the part on a hard flat surface and using the hammer very gently,

Sail winch, c1850.

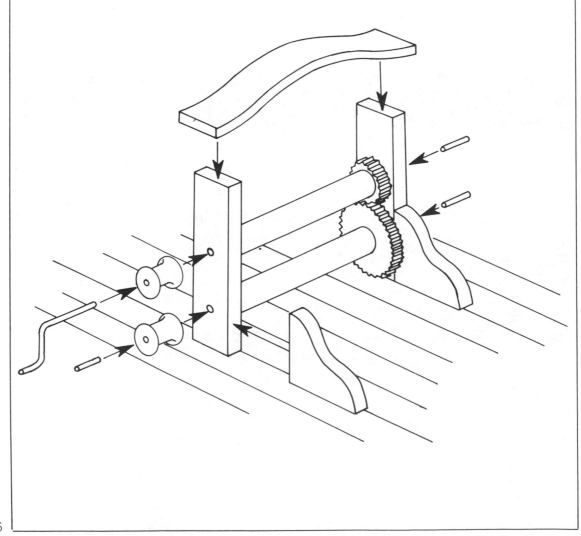

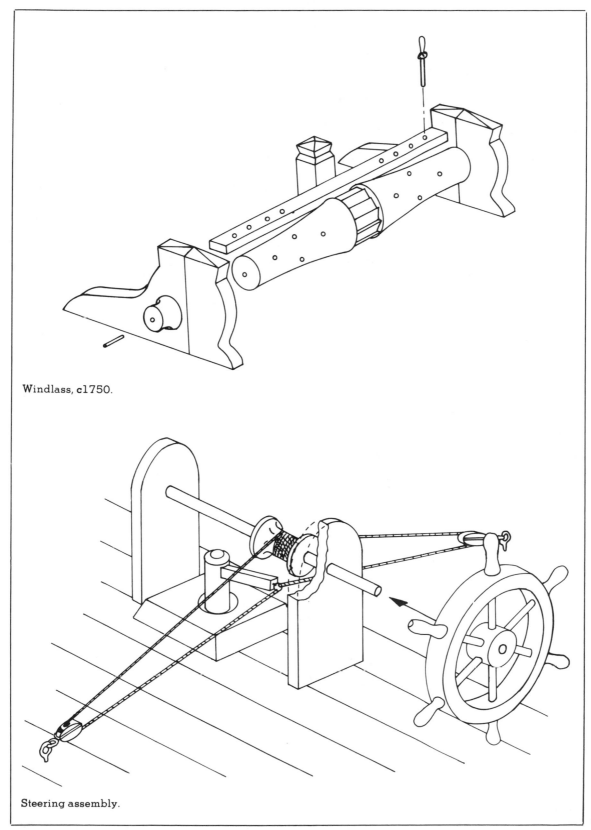

Windlass, c1750.

Steering assembly.

fit flush to the hinge, leaving the head of the pin in position. Alternatively, the part may be placed into the jaws of a vice and both sides squeezed flush. It will be noticed that no mention of glueing the parts into position has been made. Experience has shown that the parts, if assembled correctly, do not require any glue to hold them together. Once both sets of hinges are fitted, the pins connecting them should be inserted, and this operation is best completed all together. It is almost impossible to separate the rudder from the post once one pin has been fitted, without causing some distortion.

The completed rudder should be dry-fitted into position, and you should now decide whether to show a movable rudder or a static one. If a movable rudder is your choice, a hole to allow the rudder to protrude above deck level must be drilled, and the rudder top shaped to allow the fitting of the tiller. As shown, glue assembly into position, and allow to set, using the Superstick glue.

Fitting the bowsprit

This item should really be included within Chapter 8, but, because of its connection with the deck fittings in the bows, you will find it more helpful to effect the placing before the fitting of the foreward bitts.

The bowsprit should be assembled using the parts mentioned. The shaping and rigging are described in Chapter 8, and should be completed before fitting to the model. A small hole should be cut in the join of the two bulwark sides in the correct position. The angle of the bowsprit, and the position, which should be completely in line with the two masts, should be checked. If correct, carefully enlarge the hole until the bowsprit will fit. A small round file, or reamer, is the ideal tool for this work, and this operation should not be rushed.

As quite considerable strain is placed upon the bowsprit by the rigging, it is very important that the final position is strong. The method described for the fixing of the stem should be followed, drilling a small hole large enough to take a panel pin of sufficient length to secure into the deck. The resultant top hole is easily filled, and varnished, using extra bond glue to aid security of the part where it passes through the bulwarks. A bowsprit 'stop' was also fitted on some ships, to discourage any lateral (or fore and aft) movement. This may be fitted if so desired.

Note carefully the position of any ring or eyebolt needed in the hull, to provide the fixing

Steering gear.

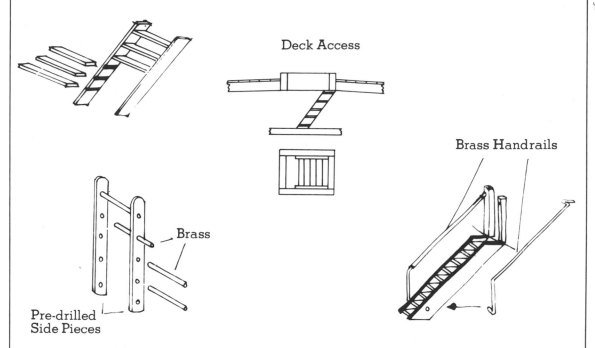

Typical Kit Ladder

Deck Access

Brass Handrails

Brass

Pre-drilled
Side Pieces

Typical ship's ladders.

Example of kit grating/hatchway combination.

points for the bowsprit rigging. These should be fitted, and as much as possible of the rigging done at this stage. This will ensure that once the 'above' deck rigging, such as the forestays, is commenced, a strong secure point is available to provide the required strain.

Ancillary equipment

Into the holes previously drilled should now be fitted the remaining small parts. These will include the belaying pins, the eyebolts and cleats. The pieces which provide a holding function, such as the eyebolts, will need the assistance of Superfast epoxy glue to avoid the part being pulled out at a critical stage.

The kit plans and instructions should be checked thoroughly to ensure all parts are in place, and, if you are satisfied, the hull should be fitted to the stand in its permanent position. Some assistance to effect this is essential to avoid the possibility of damage. The hull may now be given one or more coats of either gloss or matt varnish and allowed to dry completely. Use only thin coats, gradually building the shine to an acceptable standard, rubbing down with 'wet-&-dry' paper between each coat.

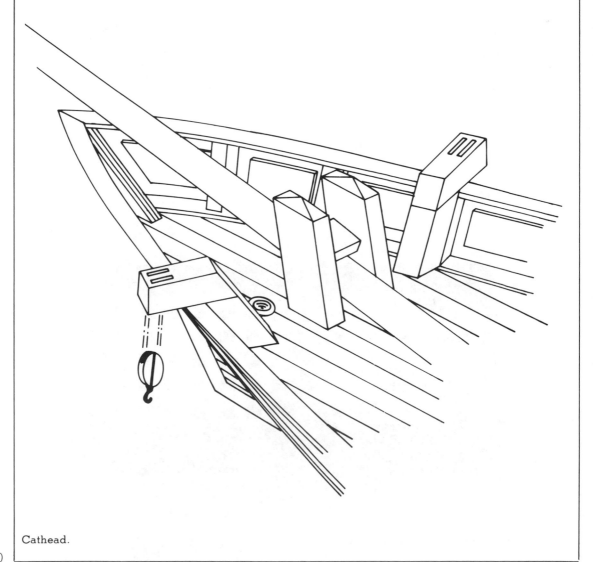

Cathead.

Anchor in stowed position. Note whipping on rope.

The completed bowsprit, rigged and in position.
Note the cathead.

The rudder assembled and ready for fitting.

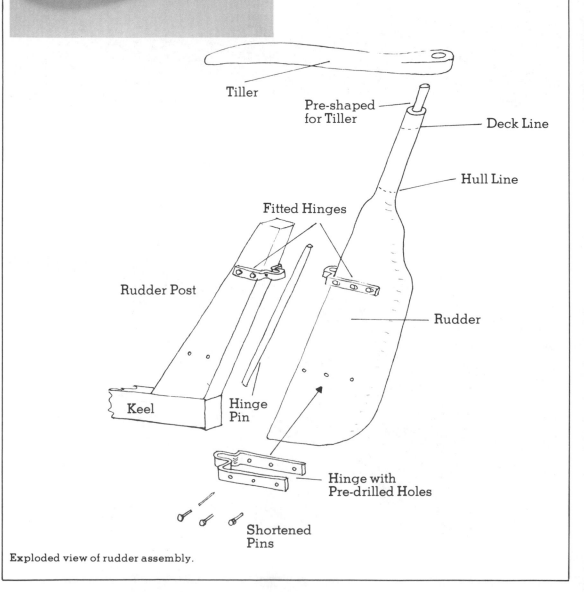

Tiller

Pre-shaped for Tiller

Deck Line

Hull Line

Fitted Hinges

Rudder Post

Rudder

Keel

Hinge Pin

Hinge with Pre-drilled Holes

Shortened Pins

Exploded view of rudder assembly.

General view of the capstan and bitts in position.
Note the rope coils on the bitts.

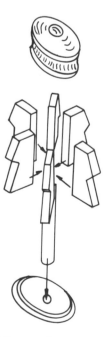

Exploded view of the capstan.

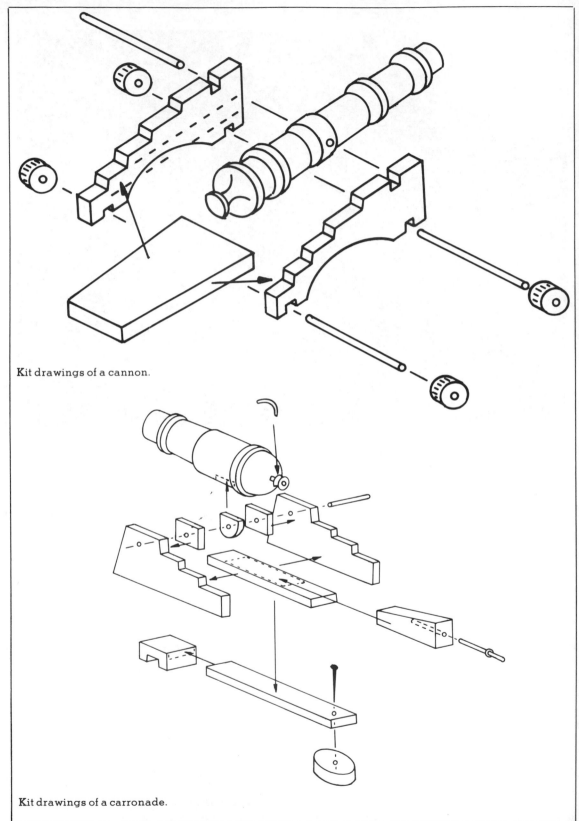

Kit drawings of a cannon.

Kit drawings of a carronade.

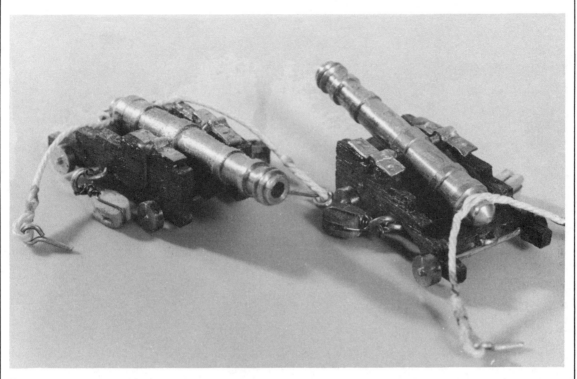

Two cannon, rigged and assembled.

The masts, yards and booms.

Chapter 8: Mast, Yards and Booms

Information and Methods

Masts on the smaller sailing vessels are usually of two types: the one piece, or 'pole', and, more commonly, two or more sections, the second section being called a 'topmast', and the upper section a 'topgallantmast'.

Cross sails were attached to the masts by means of yards and the sails which were set along the fore-and-aft line were attached by means of gaffs or booms. All yards and gaffs were moveable by means of ropes, aided by pulleys and tackles.

It is obviously to your advantage to construct

the masts and all the associated fittings **before** securing them to the model, and to make sure all the various cleats, eyebolts etc, both on the masts and on the deck are in place.

During the building stages, and after the final assembly of each mast, it is wise to check that these are, in fact, in place. For instance, once the foremast has been completed, place it in position on the model and visualise the path that the rigging will take, from the beginning of the rigging on the mast, to the final belaying pin.

It is practically impossible to effectively, and

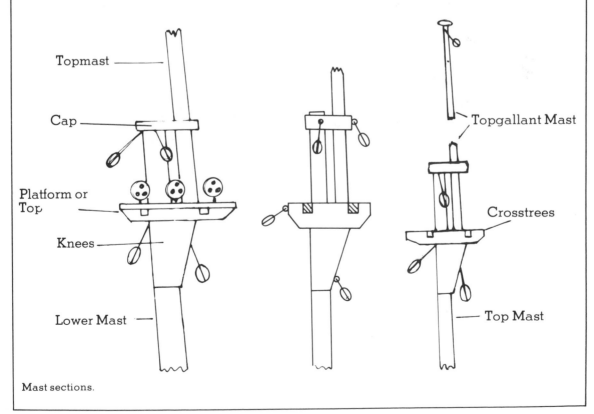

Mast sections.

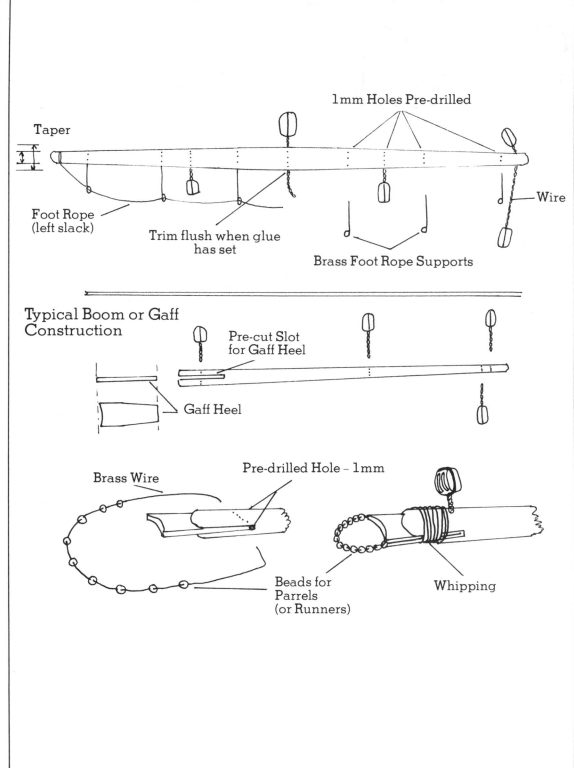

1mm Holes Pre-drilled

Taper

Foot Rope
(left slack)

Trim flush when glue
has set

Wire

Brass Foot Rope Supports

Typical Boom or Gaff
Construction

Pre-cut Slot
for Gaff Heel

Gaff Heel

Brass Wire

Pre-drilled Hole – 1mm

Beads for
Parrels
(or Runners)

Whipping

Typical kit yard fittings.

correctly, drill a hole on the model once all the rigging is in place, **so make sure the holes are accurately positioned beforehand.**

Identification of the parts

Using the measurements given within the kit, and referring to the plans, identify all the yards, gaffs and booms required for a particular mast. Cut to size, and isolate, together with the larger pieces of dowel for the mast proper. Similarly, gather all additional parts, such as the platforms, or tops, the crosstrees, knees, and all the various blocks that are fitted. Use a plastic freezer bag to keep all the parts together, suitably labelled. Repeat this operation for all the masts, and the bowsprit.

Mast construction

Step-by-step construction drawings are featured, and are of a representative type of mast. The taper of the masts and yards can be effected quite simply using a surform or file, and turning the part continuously, sanding to a smoothness. Taper and smooth each mast and yard, and lay the parts out over a flat surface, referring to the plans, to gain an idea of the location of each part.

Because of the difficulty of fitting once all the ancillary parts, such as blocks, etc. are in place, it is recommended that the fore-and-aft gaffs and booms are made and placed on the masts before the main assembly. To place the 'skid' or swivel wire, on the mast, once it is in position,

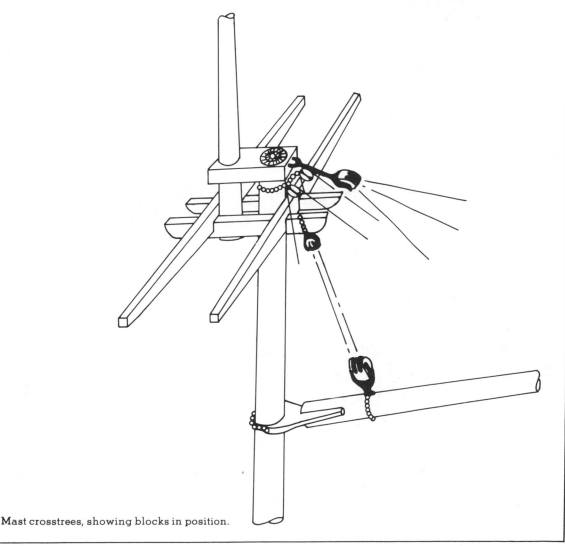

Mast crosstrees, showing blocks in position.

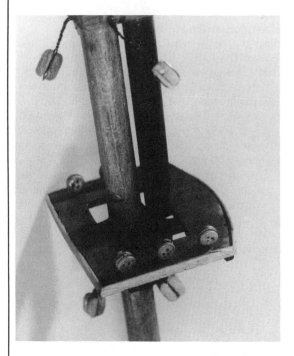

Mast table with topmast deadeyes, rigging blocks etc, in position.

is very difficult. A much neater assembly can be constructed in this manner. The part can be moved during construction, and should present no obstruction or hindrance. Also during construction, ensure that there is sufficient space between the upper and lower masts to rig the stays and shrouds. Various methods are shown for this operation, and you must decide, using the kit plans, which method suits your particular model.

Yard and boom construction

As with the construction of the masts, it is necessary to drill all the holes required for the various fittings of the yards, before starting assembly. Note carefully, using the plans, the position of each block or sheave, and mark the site. Use a dart point as before, to help locate the drill. Ensure that the holes to be drilled are all in line with one another, as a crooked angle between the blocks will be very noticeable.

The blocks may be fastened to the yards and masts by simply tying the tail of the block around the other parts. However, due to the large amount of rigging required by sailing

Boom, showing parrel beads.

Spanker sail gaff with sail. Note there is no lower
boom fitted.

Gaff, showing rigging. Note splicing on ropes.

vessels, a small model can quite often be spoilt by looking over-crowded. If you want to simulate the fixing points, you may glue a single thin strand of black cotton around the yard, over the position of the block. The holes within each block should be clear for the 'running' rigging (described in Chapter 9) and a check to make sure is time well spent.

When applying a protective coat of varnish or shellac to the mast, prior to fitting, make sure none enters the holes on the blocks and deadeyes. Being mainly constructed of boxwood, the blocks, etc, may be left without any form of protection (apart from a securing drop of glue on the tails).

It is impossible to generalise on the making of the masts and yards, etc, due to the differences in rigging which developed over the years. Many other variations are possible, and the type to be used will be ordered by the date of the ship in question, for instance, a Tudor vessel would be completely different, both in actual sizes of the parts, and in the way she was rigged, to a ship of Nelson's time. These would also be completely different to a clipper ship.

The drawings and photographs used are intended to act purely as a guide to establish the principle, and are typical of most model kits. The importance of consulting the kit plans during construction cannot be over-emphasised.

Standing rigging, before the ratlines and yards
have been fitted.

Chapter 9:
Rigging the Model

Information on rigging

The rigging on sailing ships presents, to a layman's eye, a bewildering complex of ropes, blocks, stays, etc. Yet if you remember that every single rope performs a single function, by tracing a rope from its source to its terminating point, its purpose should become apparent!

Rigging is divided into two groups: the standing rigging - ropes that do not move once in position - and the running rigging - ropes that, when pulled or moved, cause other parts on the ship to alter their position.

On any ship the standing rigging is always fitted first, to take the strain and to provide support, for the other parts to be moved by the running rigging. The heaviest (or thickest) ropes are always placed where the strain is liable to be greatest, thus the higher the rigging ascends, the thinner it becomes. This important fact is often disregarded by modelmakers and completely spoils the appearance of an otherwise beautiful model! By following a basic rule of commencing the rigging on the lower mast with the thickest thread available in the kit, and reducing in size upwards, you will not fall into this trap!

Another aspect of sailing ship rigging, frequently overlooked, is the practice of protecting the standing rigging from the effects of salt spray and water by the use of Stockholm tar. This can be represented with the use of either black waxed thread, or staining the white cotton thread (most commonly included in kits) with a mixture of matt black varnish and paint. This technique can be done either before rigging the model (staining the complete hank), or later when all the standing rigging is in place. Obviously the builder will have to exercise great care not to spill any paint, or flick the brush whilst painting the rigging in this position. Experience has taught me that the small amount of expense incurred to buy a supply of black waxed thread, of various thickness, is more than justified by both the appearance, and the time saved.

Running rigging was mainly of hemp or manilla rope, and in time, due to the salt-laden atmosphere, the original light brown colour faded to a dirty grey. For modelling purposes, any thin light brown, glazed thread, is suitable. As the running rigging is mainly for use in the blocks, etc, one thin size is usually sufficient. The glazing on the thread will ensure a smooth passage through the blocks, without the danger of snagging. The cotton thread included within the kits may be used, but needs to be treated first before use. Immerse the complete hank into a dish of either cold strong tea, or a solution of strong vinegar. Allow to soak overnight before first squeezing the excess liquid out, and stretching the hank to dry, to reduce the kinking of the 'ropes'. The greatest sin a modelmaker can commit is to rig his model with **white** thread! This is completely wrong for the ship, and would ensure a booby prize in any competition.

Preparing the blocks and deadeyes

As mentioned in Chapter 8, the holes in all the blocks and deadeyes are better cleared of obstructions, prior to fitting. Obviously when threading the running rigging, the last thing you want to come across is a jammed or blocked block. The work, though boring, is **essential**.

Use a methodical approach by transferring the cleared blocks from one container into another, clearly marked. Use a 1mm drill and

Another view of the standing rigging.

Method of securing lower deadeyes into position.
Note the simple jig to aid positioning distances.

the pin chuck (described in Chapter 11) and treat each hole in each block until the work is complete. This is one of the jobs which can be done whilst waiting for other parts to glue and set. If a power drill is available, the work is made that much easier, though greater care is needed to avoid accidents (and blood does so spoil the appearance of the wood!).

Fitting the forestays etc: hints and method
The position of the forestays are shown on the drawings. The top ends, where they fit round the mast, are usually finished in a splice for neatness. For the modelmaker to attempt this is practically impossible, on the scale of most kits. Using a very simple technique, this can, however, be simulated.

Experiment using a length of thread held with two ends between the finger and thumb. Place a small blob of carpenter's glue in between the fingers, and simply roll the two ends together. By continuous rolling, the ends will stick and the threads will be completely covered. Practice this method until confident to attempt it in any position. Even quite thick ropes can be spliced in this manner.

Fit all the various sized forestays on the mast,

Shroud and stay fitting. Note waxed thread, topmast deadeyes and splicing on ropes.

87

Forestay running rigging on bowsprit. Note the unstowed anchor and cathead rig, and the tackles on the bowsprit.

ensuring adequate length is left for the model. Similarly, measure the lengths of the lower backstays (or shrouds) taking into account the loop required for the deadeyes where it will fit at the lower end. Leave sufficient thread to be able to work comfortably, and without strain. To try to effect a neat appearance, using the barest minimum length possible, is impossible. Always allow approximately 5-8cm working length. It is far better to waste cotton than to lose patience and time, attempting the impossible!

To avoid confusion, the term deadeye refers to a standing rigging block that does not move, once in position. They were, and indeed, still are, used to tighten the stays on the mast, by means of the lacing between the upper and lower deadeyes fitted. Alternatively, especially during the era of the great clipper ship tea races, by slackening the shrouds and backstays on the masts, some captains could alter the angle of the masts. This in turn would drive the ship deeper into the water, thus reducing the amount of 'heel' or angle. Unfortunately, as these ships were most

efficient in conditions above a half gale, any sudden increase in the wind velocity, resulted in the vessel 'driving' completely under the waves, with consequent total loss of life.

To ensure the correct angle of the masts, construct a simple template, using the kit plans. When tightening the rigging, apply only sufficient tension for this angle to be reached. Refer to drawings for guidance.

Securing the blocks and deadeyes

As all the blocks and deadeyes perform a function with some degree of strain attached, you should ensure that no block or deadeye will pull out once this strain is applied. By taking this necessary precaution, confidence in the work is gained, and the necessary tautness in the rigging, so essential for a good appearance, is achieved.

Unless the builder is proficient in tying small, neat knots, these should be avoided. Practice employing the splicing method, using thread, around the blocks, until the smallest possible tail can be reached. Ensure no glue

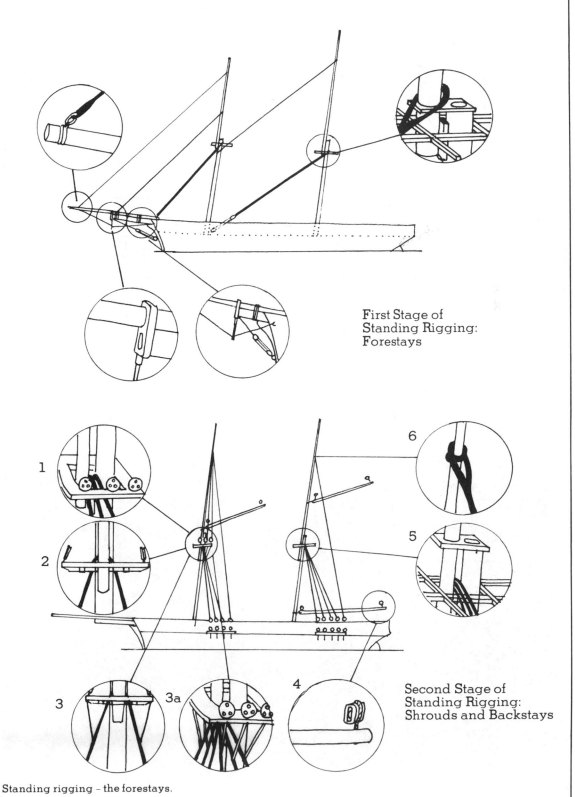

First Stage of
Standing Rigging:
Forestays

6

5

1

2

3   3a   4

Second Stage of
Standing Rigging:
Shrouds and Backstays

Standing rigging – the forestays.

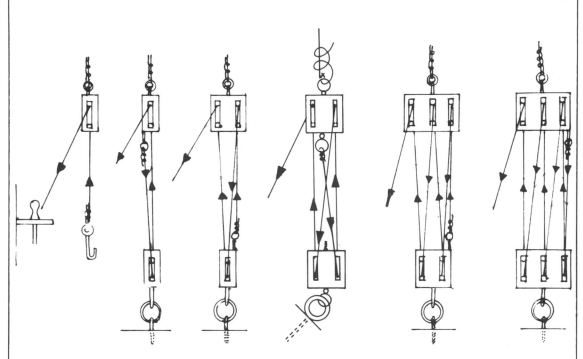

Lacing different tackles.

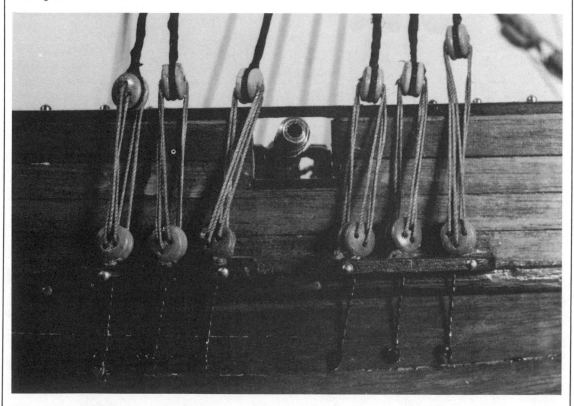

Deadeyes in position.

stops the block holes, and most important, that the block will not fall out of the loop so formed!

All the rigging blocks can be fashioned in this manner, but especially where a rigging 'tautness' is desirable, the tail can be fashioned using very thin wire. This is usually included in most kits; if not, 5 amp fuse wire will make a good strong substitute. Into a loop of wire, approximately 20mm deep, insert the block and twist the wire evenly to simulate threaded rope. When wire is used, the tail **must** be glued into the hole required using Superfast epoxy glue. Obviously no strain must be placed upon the block until the glue has set.

The blocks secured by thread can be secured into position using woodworking adhesive. In both instances, any excess tails must not be trimmed until the glues have hardened to take the strain.

Whippings

The term 'whipping' simply means to wind thread, or thin rope, around the ends of another rope to stop the rope from fraying, or to form a loop (similar to splicing).

For modelmaking purposes, due to the scale involved, accurate 'proper' whippings are not necessary. However as an alternative to splicing, you may practice if desired. The most common whipping used is the 'American' whipping. The method is explained in the drawings. It will be noticed that the two ends will be completely buried, once the tails are removed, and this ensured that, if done properly, the whipping would not come undone. It must be stressed for neatness, always use as thin a whipping thread as possible. Stocking thread is ideal!

Tackles

By using tackles (a series of pulleys) on board ship, quite enormous weights could be either moved or lifted. Generally, the greater the number of sheaves in the blocks used, the greater the pulling power.

Some combinations of blocks are shown to aid the builder, and the most important fact to be remembered is that the person pulling the end of the tackle rope would need to be on a firm footing whilst doing so. Always work out just **where** the final end will appear from the tackle. It should **always** assume a downward

All masts in line after fitting shrouds and stays.

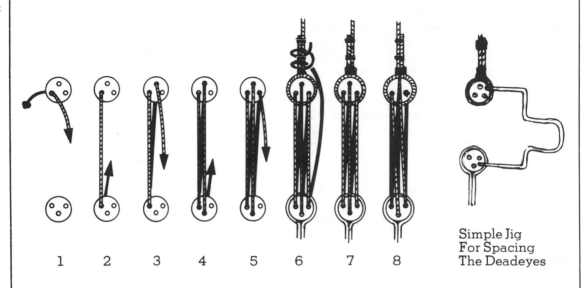

1 2 3 4 5 6 7 8

Simple Jig
For Spacing
The Deadeyes

Sequence of lacing deadeyes.

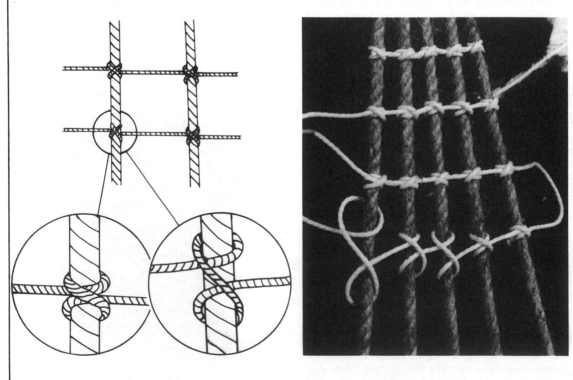

Lacing the ratlines, using a clove hitch knot.

Enlarged view of lacing ratlines.

attitude, as shown. The last part of the tackle rope is called the downhaul and this part is usually fastened to the belaying pins, or to the cleats.

Rigging the masts to the model

Assuming that you are working to the sequence described, each mast should be festooned with all the associated threads for the stays and shrouds hanging loose. In position will also be the various required gaffs and booms, but **not** any of the cross yards. All blocks, eyebolts and cleats should also be in position, **and** the mast ring which fits on the deck.

The mast rings should not be glued into position until all the standing rigging is in place, and the angles of the masts are correct. The method of achieving this will be described at a later stage. Double-check that all the eyebolts, cleats and belaying pins, are also fitted on the deck, as both difficulty and frustration will occur if they are not. Similarly, fit any blocks to the deck level eyebolts needed.

If satisfied, place the foremast into the deck hole previously drilled. Using the angled template, carefully rig the tackle, or make a loop, to fasten the lower forestay in position. Allow a very slight forward angle, to counteract the tension that will be placed upon the stay later. Place the subsequent masts into position, and repeat the operation. **Do not** glue the masts in the hole at any stage. This allows

Ratlines and lubber shrouds. Note the untrimmed ends of the ratlines.

for a slight 'side-ways' movement, if needed, to ensure the masts will be vertical to the deck, and **most important**, in line with one another. Continue to rig all the forestays on each mast, working from the bows to the stern, taking the lower stays as a guide in relation to the required tension. Ensure that no forward bend in the topmasts (denoting too much tension), occurs, as because of the complimenting effect of the rigging (one stay helps to support another), this effect will be impossible to remedy. Once all the upper and lower stays are in position, starting at the foremast, commence to rig the lower stays, or shrouds.

At the end of each shroud must be secured a deadeye which, in turn, will be laced to the ones secured into the shroud tables, already fitted. The usual position of the upper deadeyes on the stays and shrouds, was in line with, or just above, the gunwale. (Refer to the drawings and photographs.) When forming the loop to take the deadeye, the use of a simple 'jig' (as shown) will aid the positioning. Use the splicing method to secure the loops, and by careful measurement, and allowing for some

very slight stretching of the thread, place each deadeye needed for each stay in position. Allow adequate drying time **before** commencing to lace the two deadeyes for each shroud and stay.

The method of lacing is shown. Always secure the securing knot with glue and allow to dry before trimming the excess tails, using a sharp blade. **Always** work in pairs when tightening the stays and shrouds, and work from the aftermost lower shroud toward the front, at each mast. Thus the greatest counter strain to the forestays will be applied first, reducing the possibility of some stays becoming slack, as others are tightened. Refer to the drawings for instruction.

All the shroud and stay deadeyes should be in a line along the gunwale top when this operation is complete. Do not be satisfied with a gross distortion of line. If carefully done, it is quite a simple matter to 'unwind' the splice and shorten the thread by the necessary amount. The time involved will be justified by the enhanced appearance of your model.

The belaying pins in position, with one downhaul secured.

Fitting the upper shrouds

In addition to the lower, main shrouds, other shrouds were fitted from the platform (or 'top') to the next section of the mast. These were usually of thinner rope than the lower, and the deadeyes were usually smaller. Refer to the drawings for position and typical assembly. Note that the deadeyes are usually smaller, in keeping with the thinner thread used. Fitting the deadeyes can be done in several ways, as shown, and you should ensure a neat appearance whichever way is used.

The top shrouds may be fitted during the rigging of the mast, prior to fitting it to the deck. Alternatively, the shrouds may be fitted once the mast is in position. It is entirely the builder's choice. The platform deadeyes should be fitted **before** the mast is placed on the vessel, for ease of working. I personally prefer the complete fitting, because of the ease, and great manageability of the smaller parts.

The top ends of the stays are fastened to the mast quite simply. Instead of tying each shroud separately, the loops are measured approximately and gathered at the top using a single loop of thread. This is then wound around the mast and the sides of the loop gathered on each side, to make them 'sit' against the side of the mast. Refer to the drawings.

Ratlines

To enable the seamen to climb up the masts to take in the sails, etc, a series of steps were placed up the sides of the shrouds. These steps are called 'ratlines'. They commenced above the upper deadeye and continued up the shrouds to whatever height was necessary. Where the platform interrupted the ladder, the shrouds were divided. It will be seen from the drawings that added side shrouds are fitted, the main ones leading to a hole in the platform. This hole was known as the 'lubber hole'. No seaman worthy of the name would dare to climb through the 'lubber hole'; this easier passage was reserved for 'no-seaman', or 'land lubber' – hence the name.

When lacing the ratlines up the shrouds, (as shown in the drawings) complete all the main shrouds up to the lubber hole. Using the same

1. First Loops Around Pin

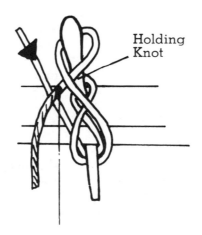

2. Trim Close to Belaying Pin

3. Separate Coil Fitted Later

Holding Knot

Method of securing downhauls and a separate coil.

thin cotton as the ratlines, lace in the added side shrouds, and complete the ratlines. The topmast shrouds should also be fitted with their ratlines. The method of tying the ratlines is shown.

The previous remarks regarding scale appearance are also applicable here. Use as thin a cotton or thread as possible. Remember that the scale figure has to step up the ratlines provided for him. Do your steps mean an easy one foot step for him? Or do they mean a step as high as a kitchen table top? or even higher? Similarly, care must be taken not to draw the shrouds together when lacing the ratlines. The ensuing bends are very unsightly.

You may find that it is easier to work by tying the ratlines working from the top of the shrouds, downwards. The previous line is visible, and the tension required is quickly found. A shortish, fairly thick needle, preferably with a wide hole, should be employed. Use only single thread, knotting at the hole.

Fitting the running rigging

Refer to the section relating to tackles, before continuing with the rigging. Commence rigging the yards to the model by threading the central lifting tackle in the middle of the yard. Do not pull the tackle completely together, leave at least 20mm distance between. Thread the downhaul through the shroud rigging to the most convenient belaying pin, or cleat. The lower yards, (which should be fitted first) may also have a length of preventer chain fitted. This was to aid the ship during times of battle, by giving the yard some protection should the tackle be shot through. If a securing loop, or skid, which allows the yard to swivel on the mast, is fitted, this should also be fitted at this time. The yard should balance with the centre tackle quite freely. If the wire has been used to provide a tail for the block, at its fitting, the height of the mast block can be adjusted later to provide tension to the tackle.

Rig the outer blocks on each yard next, leading the downhaul to a convenient belaying pin, as before. Each outer tackle must be the equal of its opposite, so ensure a straight line of the yard. Other tackles fitted to the yards must now be attached, but do **not** rig the outer adjusting tackles (called 'braces'), until **all**

yards on **all** the masts are in place.

Work from forward to aft, and after rigging the yards on the foremast, rig any gaffs or booms, on that mast before rigging the yards on the next mast. Fasten each end of the downhauls securely, and use a drop of carpenter's glue to hold. Trim the tails very closely to the pins, and finish off the appearance by providing coils of ropes on the belaying pins.

Making coils

It must be appreciated that, wherever a downhaul is fastened to a belaying pin, some length of rope would always have to be coiled as well. The coils are fashioned very easily by wrapping three or four loops of thread around either a pencil or (more easily) around a thin finger. Lightly smear a thin layer of glue over the coil, and slide the coil off the finger or pencil. While the glue is still manageable, shape the coil into an oval shape, to simulate the hanging rope shaped by its own weight. Cut off at least an inch tail, for ease of handling, and place the coil on a flat surface to dry. Fashion as many coils as are required and once set, trim off the tails.

Using a pair of tweezers, lift the top end, apply a small drop of carpenter's glue to the required site, and gently place in position. Shape finally, and allow to dry. Before commencing the final operation for the running rigging, check to ensure all parts have been fitted, no parts have been displaced, no rigging has come unwound, or untied, and no stains are present upon the decks.

Rigging the braces

The final operation in rigging the model is the fitting of the braces. It is at this point that you must decide the attitude, or angle to the ship, the yards are to take. It has been stated earlier that the yard may be trimmed, at an angle to allow the model to be placed closer to a mantlepiece or wall, or on a shelf, than if the yards are left at right angles to the ship. Another point worth remembering is that the vessel may be viewed from the side as well as from the front, and that it does help to create a different aspect of the model, from all angles.

Because the yards are moveable, the actual

View of model, showing the yards at a slight angle.

rigging should present no problems at this stage. He must, however make sure that the braces, where they terminate, are completely accessible to his 'crew'. Remember that the braces were the commonest part of the rigging to be used, and that trimming the yards to catch the wind, and so get the best sailing qualities from the vessel, was the crew's main occupation during the watches. If sails have been fitted to the model, the ropes leading from these will also have been fitted.

Protection of the rigging

Assuming that the rigging is now complete, the whole of the rigging may now be given a protective coat of varnish. Obviously to brush varnish onto all the rigging, and leave no trace would be impossible. The easy way is to enlist the help of your wife or girlfriend. Ask her to buy a tin of that particular hair-spray which leaves the hair feeling as if it has been cemented. Terrible for hair — but marvellous for models!

Stand about a foot away and spray in one long firm stroke in the general direction of the rigging. Repeat, working upwards, until the whole of one side has been covered. Turn the model around, and repeat for the other side. During this operation, the rigging may be 'teased' to form any particular curve desired, the spray ensuring the position is held. **Remember to** protect any furniture, windows, goldfish and pets during the spraying.

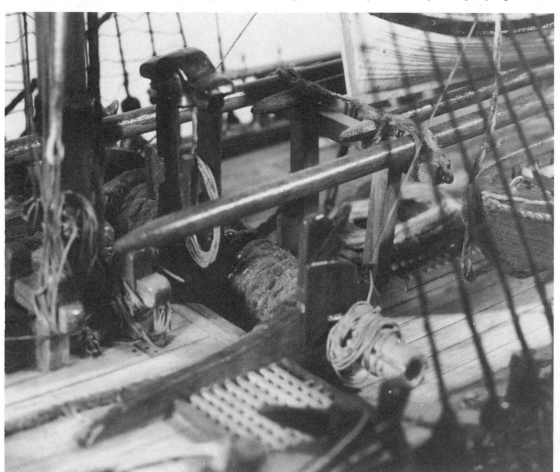

General view of another model, showing coils hung in a natural manner. Note the different thickness and texture of the ropes used, especially the anchor rope on the windlass.

Chapter 10: Stands, Sails etc.

Stands

The type of stand to be fitted to the model is always your own choice. In all cases, the priority must always be:

Appearance To have a stand which is beautifully finished and carved, may detract from the model itself! Simplicity in a stand must be a priority.

Adequate support Your stand must either have sufficient weight, or sufficient width, to provide a stable base.

Protection Not only from the model point of view, but also for the surface that the model will be displayed upon. A beautiful model which spoils the surface of a highly polished shelf will not be appreciated. Glue a piece of felt or soft cloth to the under side, if in any doubt.

Security Unless there is some special reason for the model to be able to be removed from the stand, always secure the model adequately. It may be that you will wish to enter your work in some display, or show, and in this case all the above notes are doubly applicable; in addition the model will be easier to transport.

Some types of stand, easily made, are shown. Always complete and varnish if needed before fixing to the model. If a separate name plate, or builder's name plate is

Stand with brass support pieces.

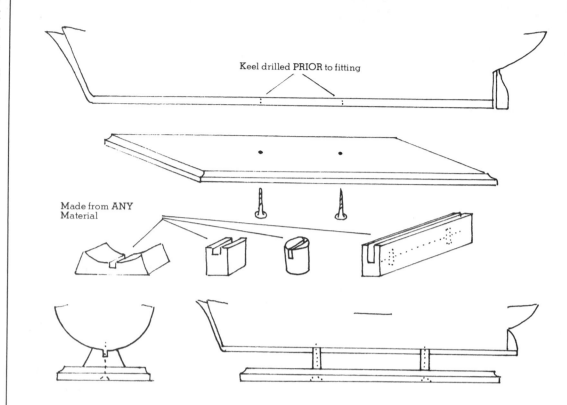

Keel drilled **PRIOR** to fitting

Made from **ANY** Material

Typical stand and supports.

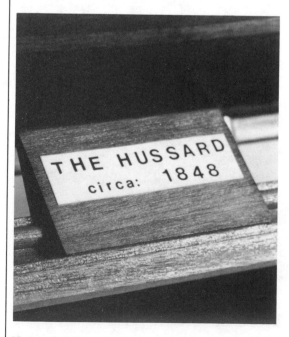

Name plate.

required, this may be made easily from either stiff card or a piece of plasticard. As before, the actual lettering should be of the Letraset type, not hand painted, unless you are skilled in this matter.

When fixing the model to the stand, to avoid any possibility of damage, enrol the help of a second pair of hands. It is practically impossible to hold a model and tighten the screws at the same time.

As described in Chapter 6, the preparation in drilling the fixing holes should be completed when fixing the keel. Only drill the keel, not the false keel, to enable a very firm joint to be accomplished. A slight smear of glue will aid the security, and always use sufficient length of screw to effect a positive join, but not so wide as to split the wood.

Display cases

If the model is to be enclosed in a display case, simplicity of design should be the prime consideration. A case with no corner pieces showing looks far more effective than one with wide, ornamented edges. More light is

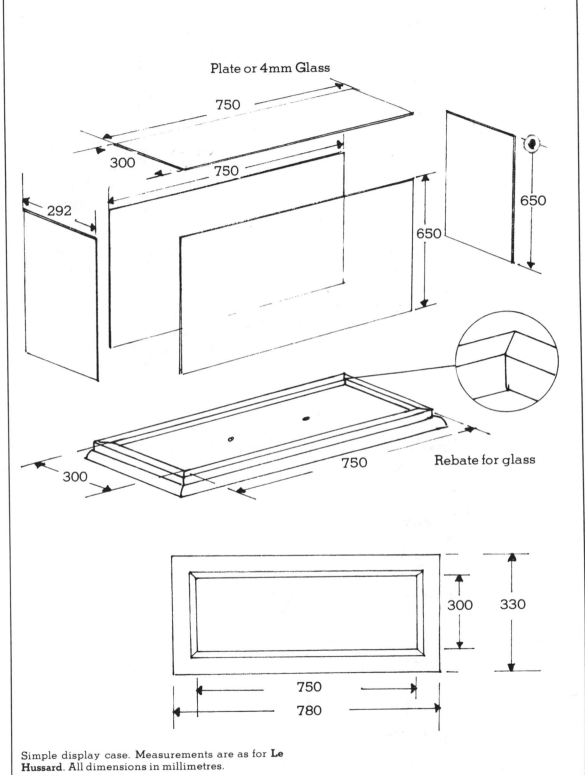

Plate or 4mm Glass

750

300

750

292

650

650

Rebate for glass

300

750

300

330

750

780

Simple display case. Measurements are as for **Le Hussard**. All dimensions in millimetres.

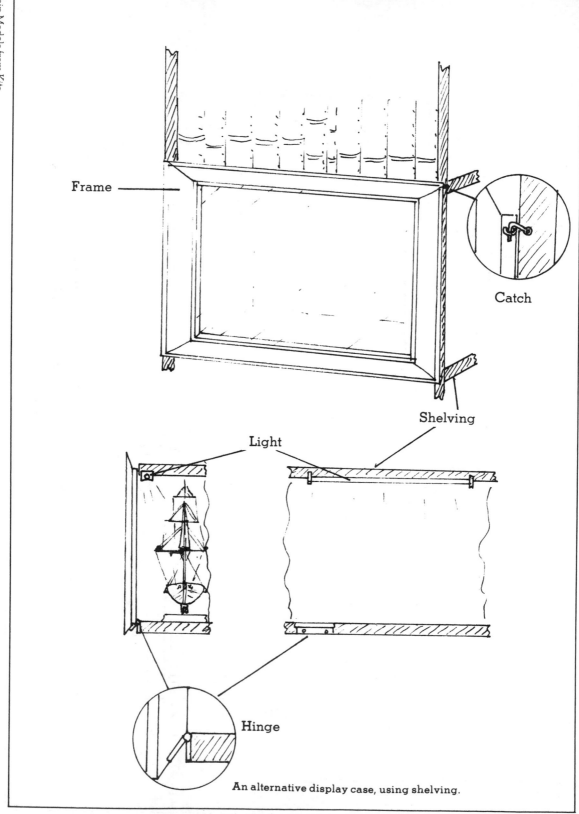

Frame

Catch

Shelving

Light

Hinge

An alternative display case, using shelving.

admitted to the subject, an uninterrupted view is possible, and the case will blend into the background.

Plain glass, accurately cut, with the edges ground and smoothed, may be used. A minimum size of 3mm is desirable for safety, and the recommended size, both for weight and appearance, is 4mm. There is less stress applied to the glass when fitting, with the reduced possibility of cracks and splintering. If the question of expense is not uppermost, use plate glass. The refraction within the glass is less, and the distortion thus caused is reduced to almost nothing.

The base of the case is constructed quite simply, incorporating an edging strip around the full base, as shown. The glass will fit within this edge, and, once the sealant is applied, will provide a dustproof join.

The sealant is a white silicon rubber, as used in the construction of fish tanks, etc. By applying a length of the rubber down one edge of the glass and pressing another panel to it, a tight bond will be affected. Because of the flexible nature of the material, the edges of all the panels may be adjusted to ensure a perfect 90 degree angle at the joins. Construct the case on a hard, flat surface, not in the base. Place all four side panels into position and allow at least 24 hours to set. **Do not** attempt to remove the overspill caused by the pressure of the joins, until the time has elapsed.

The rubber will be found to have solidified to such an extent that, using a sharp knife or razor blade, the residue may be sliced away very easily. The inside of the case should also be carefully cleaned to remove any finger marks or smears, before fitting the top panel to the four sides. If the top panel has been cut as per the drawings shown, there will be sufficient overlap for the top to fit flush to the sides and to provide a very strong join once the sealant has set. Allow the same time as before, then remove the surplus and clean the inside of the top panel.

Secure the model into the base, using screws, and apply a thin coating of sealant to the inside of the base. Press the complete case firmly into the coating, until the case is seated. Allow to dry, and clean the glass gently. If at some future time the model has to be removed, by inserting a sharp thin blade into the join at the top panel, it will be found that the seal can be broken very easily. To replace, simply clean all the old sealant away, and replace using fresh material. Because of the flexible properties of this method, the case will resist cracks and stress, and will be found to be completely dustproof.

An alternative display case

This alternative to the full display case may be considered.

A convenient corner of the room, an unused shelf within a unit, the top shelf of a china cabinet – these are ideal places where a model may be displayed to its full advantage. If a small light can also be fitted as well, the model can become a focal point in any room, instead (as sometimes happens) of a 'nuisance', especially when dusting or cleaning. You should explore every possibility to make your work an acceptable part of the decor. The drawings show a way of using existing space.

Assume the shelf is at least above waist height, and of sufficient length and depth to house the model comfortably. Construct a single surround to the space available. Blend the outside of the surround with the existing area, using the same shade of wood, for example. Cut a single sheet of glass to fit the surround and (having in mind easy removal), fit a pair of hinges to the bottom of it, with securing catches to the top. The surround should fit flush to the shelfing, or unit, to provide a dust free space.

Explore the possibilities of lighting the model, especially if the area is dark. A convenient power point, incorporating an easily accessible switch, and ensuring the light shines downwards onto the model, not outwards preventing a viewer's appreciation, is required.

This type of case can be fitted using a wide variety of materials. For instance, in a library, an antique setting might be suitable (search antique shops for an old, large, 'scroll' picture frame). Suitably lit, this type of setting can look very impressive! In a more modern setting, polished aluminium framing (of the double glazing type) can look very attractive, especially with a dark Sapele grained wood for a background.

You have a wide variety of materials and

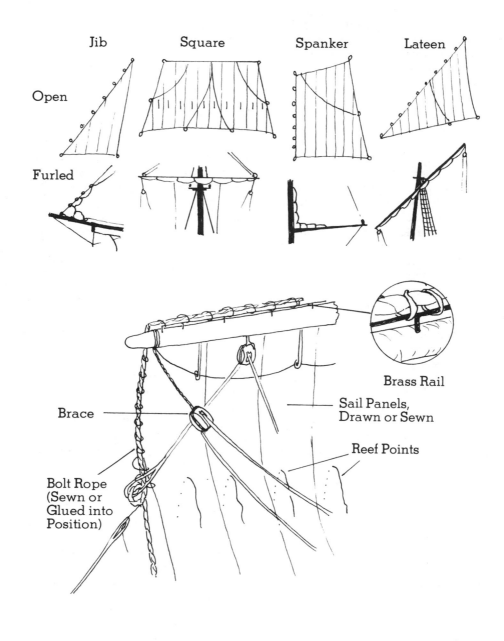

Jib Square Spanker Lateen

Open

Furled

Brass Rail

Brace

Sail Panels,
Drawn or Sewn

Reef Points

Bolt Rope
(Sewn or
Glued into
Position)

Sails, open and furled, and fitting the bolt rope.

Bolt rope on the edge of the sail, and the sail rigging
and reef points.

settings at your disposal, and your model can
be used to compliment any room. Care must
be exercised in the choice of materials used,
however. The natural tones of the wood used in
the model should blend, rather than contrast,
with the surround. Even the choice of wattage
for the light should be appreciated. A very
bright, stark light may not be ideal, when used
in conjunction with the existing lights in the
room.

These aspects must be considered, and, if
they are the final result will be acceptable to all.

Sails

The decision whether to fit sails to a model, is
yours. Some models look very attractive with a
full 'suit' others not so! Some may look far better
with the sails 'furled' (or wrapped) around the
yards, others are better with no sails at all. One
view is "If it's in a sea, put sails on it, if not –
don't!"

The usual parts of a sail are shown on the
drawings, and, to aid authenticity, these parts
should be represented to some degree. For
instance, the panels which make up the sail,

Combination of open and furled sails displayed on
another model.

may be drawn – or stitched on – using a very thin cotton, with the aid of a sewing machine. Equal spacing is essential for this operation, and the seams should be placed no nearer than 25mm apart, otherwise the impact of the seam will be lost in the scale (refer to previous notes on deck planking). Around the full edge of each sail, is a 'bolt' rope. This gives the sail strength to resist splitting, and in the model's case, can be used to give the sail the required degree of curvature by smearing with a minute touch of glue, and gently bending the sail as it sets, without creasing. Note the amount of ropes attached to the sail to enable the initial 'shortening' to be carried out from the deck; seamen only ventured onto the yard, using the foot-ropes, once this had been done. The bolt rope may be attached to the back of each sail using glue, or hand-stitched to the edges. The builder must be extremely careful to keep to the scale appearance when attempting this, otherwise a bulky, heavy-looking sail will detract from the otherwise fine appearance of the model.

Sails may also be arranged using a hair-spray, and shaping the sail whilst spraying. Remember that the sails have to be fitted to the yards **before** fitting the yards to the masts. It is virtually impossible to rig the sails neatly, and correctly, with the yards in position. An added disadvantage to fitting sails, and one that should most certainly be considered, is the amount of dust that will adhere to them! Models with sails **must** be enclosed in a completely dust-free case. Another point worth remembering is, if sails are fitted, they will hide all the rigging ropes, shrouds, ratlines and delicate work, of which you will feel a justifiable pride. The choice is yours!

THE HUSSARD
circa: 1848

Details of the after end of the hull.

Chapter 11:
Tools and Equipment

The following tool list is not intended as definitive. Suffice to say that, using the tools described, the model shown within this book was built as a prototype model for a kit in order to add any recommendations that were felt necessary, before the production run.

If you are fortunate enough to possess tools or equipment that will aid your workmanship, you will, of course, use them.

Working base board.

Tools

A pair of long-nosed pliers such as X-acto F7504.

A pair of side cutters such as X-acto F7505

A small-headed light hammer or 'toffee' hammer

A set of watchmaker's screwdrivers, the ends to be filed to a point

An electrical screwdriver, filed and honed for use as a chisel

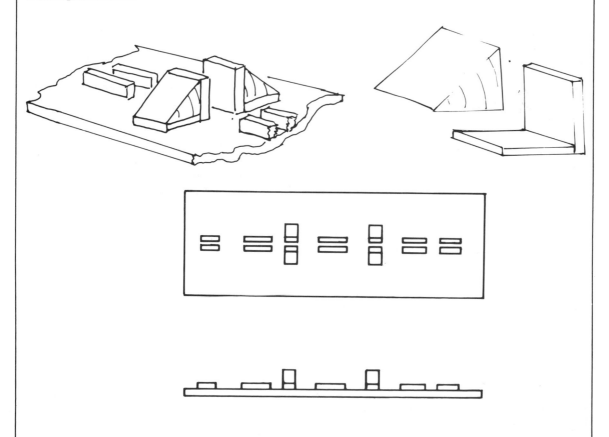

A dart head, filed to a thin point, for pinning the planks

A set of needles, or key-hole files, of differing shapes

A junior hack or jig saw, with a quantity of new blades

A broad cutting knife, such as a Stanley knife, for heavy work

A fine cutting knife such as an X-acto F3201 and spare blades

A pin vice, or chuck such as X-acto F7322 for small drill bits

A set of small drills from $\frac{1}{32}$in upwards

A table-top vice, screw fitting to the under-side of a table

A steel rule, or a sharp steel edge for straight cutting of parts

A set of small 'G' clamps such as X-acto F7450

A surform or fine rasp file

A selection of long and short tweezers

The full range of X-Acto tools is shown in the X-Acto Catalogue, available from most retailers, or from Humbrol Ltd, Marfleet, Hull, East Yorkshire.

Equipment

The equipment mentioned was used throughout the building of the model shown within this book. It is based on the assumption that the modelmaker would have to 'pack up' after each period of building. The kit box and lid can be utilised for this purpose, or a separate box used, especially for the smaller pieces mentioned.

A 2ft x 2ft working board, upon which the bulk of the building will take place, to avoid damage to table-tops. Any plywood of a medium thickness is satisfactory, from 4mm to 10mm.

A smaller, thicker piece of plywood, 6in x 6in x ⅝in, for use as a cutting board, which will help to preserve the cutting edge of the modelling knives.

A working base board, approximately 6in x 12in, used during the initial building of the hull as a 'jig' to avoid warping.

Sanding blocks of various lengths and widths, easily made from any scrap wood, together with different grades of either, sand, emery or glass papers.

Medium and fine grade 'wet-&-dry' paper, used during the varnishing sequences.

A quantity of spring-loaded clothes pegs, used as clamps.

A quantity of rubber bands, used to provide tension during glueing.

A quantity of thin, flexible copper or brass wire, to aid the positioning of parts during glueing.

The use of a steam iron, the base to be cleaned after use.

The use of a soldering iron, used to bend smaller parts.

A table-top vice.

Paints, either matt or gloss enamels, as required.

Varnishes, either matt or gloss polyurethane clear.

Clear shellac, if preferred.

Wood stains, as required.

White spirit or turpentine substitute, for cleaning brushes etc.

A quantity of brushes of varying thickness and texture.

Additional cards of black, waxed thread, if required.

Additional bobbins of blazed, mid-brown thin threads.

A good quality section of distinctive grained wood to form the model stand (approximately 12in x 5in).

A good quality section of wood, with distinctive grain, to form the display case base (approximately 32in x 13in).

Felting, to provide an anti-scratch base under either the display case or the model stand.

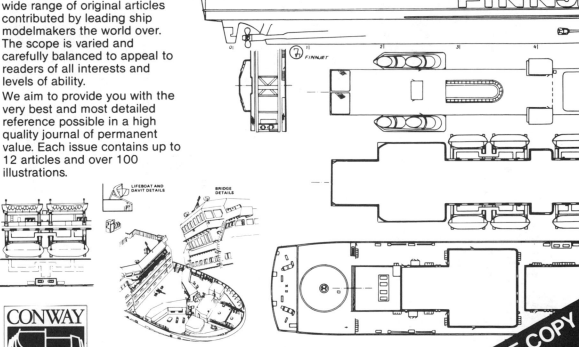
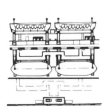

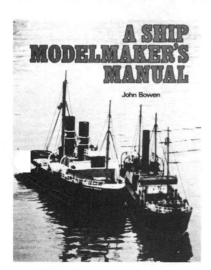
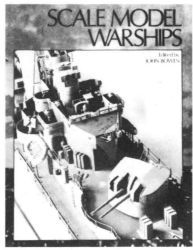
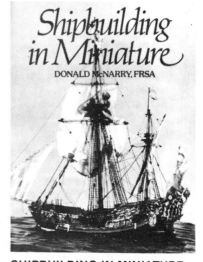